THE CHAMPION'S WAY

Core Foundations for Achieving Peak Performance in Sports and Life

VERONICA KARAMAN

The Champion's Way
Core Foundations for Achieving Peak Performance in Sports and Life

Authors note: Some of the names of the individuals in the student stories have been changed to protect their privacy.

For information about special discounts for bulk purchases, contact us at: www.truechampioncoaching.com

ISBN: 978-0-578-58753-0

To all aspiring athletes and high performers
who seek to release the champion within.
I believe in you.

To all coaches and parents looking for a
better way to train and nurture your athletes.

To every seeker of greatness wondering how
to win from a place of love and acceptance.

In memory of my mother, a great athlete
who never discovered her full potential
but gave me a joyful glimpse of it.

The Champion's Way

Contents

The Champion's Way

THE CHAMPION'S WAY

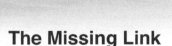

The Missing Link

There is a missing link in the area of peak performance training. Athletes and other high performers have access to all kinds of cutting-edge resources equipping them to maximize their potential. From specialized fitness trainers to nutritional coaching to ground-breaking knowledge in neuroscience, we have made great advancements in maximizing human potential.

It is now common for a rising competitive athlete to have an entourage of coaches. A young golfer is not fully equipped unless he has a swing coach, a fitness coach, a mental game coach, and a nutritional coach. A lesson is not complete without a training video and feedback from a computer on launch angles.

When I was growing up, I had a golf instructor, a bag of practice balls, a golf course, and a deep hunger to improve. That's it! I had to learn how to play the game myself. I had to learn how to think, compete, and master all the elements by becoming self-efficacious. Self-efficacy is a term I learned when I was a PhD student. It basically means "self-motivated learning." I had to teach myself. I had to embrace my own desire to be a champion and develop my own self-awareness without a machine or another voice telling me what to do. In other words, my learning was driven from within.

While I appreciate and embrace all the resources for developing a champion today, I see a missing piece of knowledge that is imperative for a competitor if he's to excel. It is the knowledge of what peak performance is, how it happens, and what its components are.

The Champion's Way is a training manual that provides a simple GPS system for achieving one's highest potential in a healthy, progressive way. It's a framework of thought. Once a high performer starts equipping with it, he will take a significant leap in his performance. I can attest to seeing most of my students who apply *The Champion's Way* enjoy results beyond their expectations, and in record time.

I also believe that the other missing piece in the peak performance equation is the role of identity. One simply cannot perform beyond how she sees herself. It's impossible. For that reason, I always begin with an inside-out approach, starting with how you see yourself.

In short, *The Champion's Way* is a way to "think about your thinking." It lays down tracks in your mind as to how to approach peak performance integrating your entire self into the process of becoming your best. It includes the physical, mental, emotional, and spiritual dynamics to achievement. It's an integrated and holistic approach. It's also deeply relational.

Besides my professional training in this area, the manual is also the result of my fifty years of thrashing through the woods of peak performance to discover some simple and clear pathways to keep growing and advancing along the road to championship in my sport of golf.

I've achieved and crashed many times. I've had successes and many failures. I've started and stopped too many times to mention. I've been in tip-top shape, and I've struggled through seventeen years of chronic fatigue. I've experienced the joys of winning and the self-destructiveness of losing. I've been honored with the celebrity of being a professional athlete. I've also experienced the destructiveness and emptiness of pursuing sport as an idol.

Today, I am free, whole, and passionate about sharing what I've learned with others, like you, to empower your way. Hopefully, your ride will be smoother! I believe as you become equipped with *The Champion's Way*, you'll love the journey down the road to championship as a means of continual self-development, self-love, and deep personal transformation.

It will help you to win, but more importantly, *The Champion's Way* will help you to get the win from within. To me, it's the win from within that makes you a true champion. In fact, I'd like to share a testimony of a true champion student who validates my point about "the missing ingredient."

A few years ago, I conducted a workshop for a group of aspiring young lady golf pros. Each player was there because of her desire to be a champion—not only to be the best she could be—but the best all around. At the end of the training, each thanked me for the valuable information she learned.

I knew each of them needed the knowledge I was presenting. However, one stepped out to possess the knowledge for herself. She was hungry for more. Elaine signed up for peak performance coaching with me, and we quickly got to work. She was in a rut and was stuck shooting around 80, which was not her norm.

When I went out on the golf course to watch her play, I noticed right away that she possessed all the skill in the world to win. I said to her, "Girl, you should be winning! Why aren't you winning?"

She was a gifted athlete and aspiring pro, but she didn't know how peak performance happens. As I mentored her in *The Champion's Way*, we worked on two key areas: educating her in defining her ideal performance state so she could intentionally "get in the zone" and helping her develop a winning mindset. I provided her with a process to connect her head and her heart, strengthening her belief in herself as a winner and champion. This was important, as she needed an identity upgrade from being a college golfer to a professional.

In less than two months' time, Elaine won her first professional championship, shooting a career best 66 on the final day. Just a few weeks' later, she won her second event. Shortly thereafter, she won her third professional tournament!

While she had the tools for playing, she needed the knowledge of peak performance and how it happens from the inside out. She is now on her way, advancing down the road to championship.

In this training manual, I use my speaking voice in my writing. I am addressing you personally and directly as if I were sitting across the table coaching you one-on-one. It's not meant to be theoretical, but practical. I want to activate your inner champion and equip you to become more and to achieve greater results.

It is my heart and aim for you to advance down the road to championship. Whether you're a parent, a coach, a businessman, an athlete, or student, *The Champion's Way* is a personal operating system that will equip you to be the champion you were created to be!

Praise for *The Champion's Way*

We have no words to express our gratitude for Veronica Karaman and *The Champion's Way*. Through Veronica's coaching and approach to peak performance, our boys, Justus and Jordan, have learned to play like champions.

When we first met Veronica, we were desperate as a family. We were stuck and needed outside help. The game we loved so much was taking its toll not only on our twin boys, but on us as a family.

Golf has been very much a part of our boys' lives for years. We started them in tournaments when they were eleven years old. They loved it and had a talent for it. You could see it in their swings— and their eyes—at this young age. However, as they were getting older, the pressure to perform mounted. It was so easy for them to equate their identity with their scores.

We could see the potential destruction of their misplaced value. Even though they were young men with great character and dedication to the game, we wanted them to be healthy competitors whose interests, sport, and faith were integrated. It was our aim to raise true champions free from the negative consequences of pursuing the love of a game at all costs.

We came to realize that if a rising player is super talented and has an ability to dominate at a high school level with sights on playing college golf, the pressure to perform intensifies with every competition. People start watching scores, and that's all they see. They see scores and rankings, and they base scholarships on these two factors. Then, when you are from a more remote state like Montana, as we are from, you don't get to go to fifteen tournaments a year. That makes the pressure of the five you play in mean even more. The stress we were feeling became overwhelming. We knew something needed to be done.

The breaking point of our stress and the thought of just walking away from the game for a season was the starting point of our breakthrough work with Veronica. We believe Veronica was the answer to our prayers for help. What we actually received through *The Champion's Way* was so much greater than what we initially anticipated.

The training provided us a fresh start and perspective. We learned a common performance language as a family to discuss our sons' play from a more objective place. The modules provided the boys with material they could review and apply on their own. The four champion zones broadened our perspective on how peak performance happens.

We saw how our paradigm for performance was stalled in the physical zone. We thought improvement was simply a matter of working harder on their swing, and wondered why we weren't getting better results. We didn't know performance takes place in four zones, not just one. When our paradigm was expanded to include the physical, mental, emotional, and spiritual zones, the entire trajectory of our sons' games took off!

The boys began to take ownership of their thoughts, emotions, reactions, and strategy for winning in a new way. They had a clear process of becoming mentally tough and debriefing their rounds on their own. The champion mindsets and identity formation helped them grow personally, too. They were able to integrate their sport and their higher purpose for play. We have seen the power of excelling in all four zones. I've even seen my one son shoot a 67 when his swing was off, but the other three zones were on.

The boys have been able to continually get closer and reach more of their potential. This year they played like champions! The champion zones are vital, and *The Champion's Way* works! Never would we have dreamt that as freshmen, they would make varsity on an AA school. After a twenty-one year deficit, they led the Bozeman Hawks to a state championship win! Not only that, Justus placed first and Jordan placed second overall. They also won All State, and broke the all-time scoring record in the state! Jordan also won the MVP award.

Let's go bigger! Never would we have dreamt that college coaches such as Oregon State, Arizona State, and University of Central Florida would be looking at them. Veronica's fingerprints are all over what they accomplished.

It's only just begun.

Most importantly, our family dynamics shifted. While we were thrilled with the new knowledge we were learning and applying to get winning results, *The Champion's Way* even surpassed all our expectations in what it did to help us as a family enjoy the game together. Our sport is fun again!

We recommend *The Champion's Way* to every athlete and high performer who wants to reach his or her potential. So many players who take their sport seriously have a limited understanding of peak performance. They only see performance through the eyes of the physical, as we once did. There are three more zones! To play from a place of limited understanding is to play your sport with one arm. To understand and apply all four champion zones is of absolute importance for anyone endeavoring to be a champion. You can't get to your potential by functioning in only one zone.

The Champion's Way brought the enlightenment and encouragement we needed to stay fully engaged in the sport we love. To see Justus and Jordan play like the true champions we desire them to be is thrilling. We are no longer desperate, but delighted to see our sons swing into their full potential.

You will, too, as you learn and apply *The Champion's Way*.

Travis and Teresa Verge,
Proud parents of Jordan and Justus Verge

THE CHAMPION'S WAY

MODULE 1

Introduction: An Inside Out Approach

Welcome to *The Champion's Way: Core Foundations for Achieving Peak Performance in Sports and Life*. As a peak performance coach and golf professional who has been a high-level competitor my entire life, I'm delighted to have you in this training. My goal is to release your champion identity and potential. We are going to go on an amazing journey together. I'll be training you in how peak performance happens, instilling champion mindsets in you, and providing motivation for excellence to empower you along your competitive journey.

I've had the pleasure of seeing amazing results with my students. One twelve-year-old student wanted to be an academic champion. In applying the principles of full engagement in *The Champion's Way*, he excelled greatly. He improved his GPA from a 2.2 to a 3.9 in just twelve weeks. A competitive junior golfer came to me shooting 88. When she applied *The Champion's Way* system, after only three weeks, she shot a career-best 76, finishing third in her state championship. Then there was an eighty-five year-old senior citizen who was given six months to live. Through *The Champion's Way* system of releasing potential and life turnaround, she lived almost seven more years. That woman was my own mother! I'm going to share that story with you later in this training.

It's an honor and a privilege for me to be able to take this training and my own personal experience to provide you with a holistic approach to peak performance.

By way of introduction, I want to set the stage with our training by sharing the approach and the philosophy of *The Champion's Way*. The best way I know how to do that is to open with a story from my own upbringing.

When I was five years old, my father placed a putter in my hand. I grew up in Western Pennsylvania, in Pittsburgh. On weekends, my dad and I would make the forty-five-minute trip from our home to Latrobe Elks Golf Club. Dad would play golf for four hours, and I would go putt for four hours straight—at six years old! Either I was crazy, or I had a passion. Putting was something I just loved to do.

We belonged to a fraternal organization. Every summer our family would arrange our vacations around the national golf tournament the organization held. My father entered me into their national peewee putting contests. For nine years straight, it would be my summertime passion to play in the peewee putting contests that I was determined to win!

When I turned fourteen, I was too old for the age bracket to putt. The only way I could continue to putt was to take up the whole game of golf. I became a serious competitor in my late teens. That's when I began to focus on competing, achieving, and winning.

Here are two pictures from the young days of my amateur career that represent the essence of what *The Champion's Way* is all about. I'm six years old here (left). You can see the putter is almost as tall as I am. There's a little trophy in my hands. This picture represents passion.

Here's the other picture (right), when I was eighteen. I was playing in The West Penn Amateur, in the heat of competition. You can see that this picture represents focus. You can just look at my eyes and see the "eyes of the tiger."

According to sports psychologist Dr. David Cook, there are two distinguishing features of champions. One is passion, and the other is focus. Focus is the ability to direct your mind to a target. Passion is love for the game.

Anytime you can open up your mind to discover a new possibility for yourself, allowing your passion and motivation to come out while concurrently maintaining superior focus, you will take a leap in your performance.

Everything that we're doing in *The Champion's Way* will be about increasing your passion and focus. This involves finding processes, mindsets, and practices to release your passion and increase your focus. Once you apply these strategies, you'll see your performance improve.

The reason this particular approach to performance training is important is because I believe there is a champion in everyone. I believe there's a champion in you!

So often we say, "When I win the tournament, when I get the trophy, when I achieve my result, then I'm a champion." The beauty of *The Champion's Way* is that right now you're a champion. Consider the following analogy that demonstrates this truth:

Picture a full-blown apple. It's not going to get any more developed than when fully ripe. Now consider an apple seed. If you look at the seed next to the full-blown, ripe apple, there's no difference between them in terms of their DNA. The little seed contains everything about  being an apple that there is to contain. The only thing missing is time and the right nurture—the sun, the soil, the nutrients—for the seed to grow into a full-blown apple.

Maybe you're ten years old just starting on your competitive journey. You're feeling like a seed, but you sense something stirring inside that wants to be a champion. Perhaps you're a teenager who's tasted some victory and wants to get even better. Or, you may be a full-blown, developed champion who simply wants to shine a little brighter. Wherever you're on the road to championship, you are already a champion—and we are going to release more of the champion within you!

In *The Champion's Way*, we focus on personal growth; that is, personal development from the inside out. We're going to develop the champion inside of you to experience peak performance on the outside of you. That's the way we're going to create success from the start.

 The inside-out approach doesn't begin with results or scores, but values. Values are important. They're the root system enabling you to grow into your full potential. They define who you are and what's important to you. Values are the invisible anchors that shape your decisions and keep you solid and centered. Your scores will come and go—they vacillate like the ever-changing weather. Values keep you grounded.

As we develop an approach to peak performance that's inside-out, we'll begin with who you are as a champion. There are five core values we want to develop on the road to championship.

The Five Core Values of *The Champion's Way:*

The first value is *P for Potential*. Everyone has untapped potential. I don't care if you're ten years old and just starting on your road to championship. I don't care if you're eighty and you feel like it's about over for you. Everyone has untapped gifts and talents. We want to release those gifts and abilities within you.

Here's the key to releasing potential: You can only start from where you are. You can't start from where you are not. As we embark on this training journey together, I want you to start from a place of acceptance. You may feel like an average athlete or student. You may feel like a budding champion already who's on the verge of greatness. It doesn't matter. We're going to start where you are and release your potential without comparing yourself to anyone else.

The second value is *R for Results*. We want to create results for you. These are going to be personal growth-driven results, whether you want to win a tournament, your competitive season, or simply achieve a personal goal. We want to see results from the energy you invest in releasing your potential and from the knowledge that you're gaining.

The third value is *E is for Excellence*. I'm absolutely amazed at how many people in our culture have no standard of excellence. They're caught up in mediocrity, doing whatever they have to do just to get by. Success comes from a determined state. There must be something inside you that wants to tap the most out of who you are. There has to be a deep desire to find out what is on the inside of you. There has to be a high standard of excellence to realize your potential. I want you to be a champion of excellence. These are the top three values: potential, results, and excellence.

The fourth value is **W for Wholeness**. Wholeness is important because we want to develop the whole person. This has to do with the integration of who you are as a competitor, an athlete, an achiever, and also a human being who relates, loves, and connects with people. The "doing and being" sides of you must come together in harmony for you to be a healthy competitor. We want to create a holistic approach to peak performance. You want to develop into a whole person who is a fracture-free competitor. Remember, you are not your score!

Why is this important? I've spent a lot of time achieving and crashing in my life. I went through a long season where I struggled through seventeen years of chronic fatigue. I had to work through what was inside of me that was driven to achieve, but then I crashed and burned. I came to realize that I needed both the "being" and the "doing" side of me developed. I'm glad I am now healed and able to help others to avoid the same pitfalls I experienced as a highly driven achiever who was too performance-oriented.

The development of *The Champion's Way* has not only come from my training and experience in peak performance, but also from my failures. My development came from the things that knocked me down and out, and the places where there was no one to help me understand why I got that result. I figured a few things out in the process. I want to bring that foundation to you, so that as you travel along your road to championship, you can become fracture-free. You can be a whole person.

The last value is **F for Freedom**. Freedom is the ability to express yourself, your personality, and your individuality freely. Often athletes think the only thing they can do is play their sport. They don't realize that they could also be an author, a speaker, a businessman, or a musician as well.

You look at somebody like Arnold Palmer, who was an amazing golfer. He was also a father, a businessman, a philanthropist, and a golf course architect. You could say the same for Jack Nicklaus. He too had freedom to be the whole person that he was created to be.

As we go along this journey, I want you to have the freedom to be yourself.

As I work with a lot of competitive junior golfers, I realize that there are some who are power-driven. It's in their essence to want to get up and whack the ball, and they are all about power. That's who they are. I encourage them to be free to express their uniqueness.

There are some I call thinkers and reflectors. I've got one student I call the wise owl. Her giftedness is to be able to strategically think through a championship. The wise owl is not going to be like the power chick. They each have the freedom to express and develop who they are in their own uniqueness.

These five core values are foundational to *The Champion's Way* process of development. They form the inner core of a champion. Nurturing these values will help you bloom into the person you were created to be—along with the competitor, the athlete, and the achiever you aspire to be.

If you put the first letters together from each of the five values, you get the word "PREWF," pronounced "proof." The values are P-R-E-W-F: Potential, Results, Excellence, Wholeness, and Freedom. Implementing them will be the proof of your champion development.

The Champion's Way is all about creating superior values and results. One of the greatest tenets of *The Champion's Way* is that performance plus relationship equals wholeness. Life can't all be about performance, and it can't all be about relationship. It's the two working together, with both parts supporting one another. The best way to achieve is to create "performance from relationship" to become the true champion you were designed to be.

Who Is *The Champion's Way* for? I'm a golf professional, and much of my experience has been with competitive golfers. If that's you, this course is definitely for you, but it goes beyond golfers. *The Champion's Way* lays a foundation for peak performance for any kind of athlete in any sport. If you've got a ball, and you want to get it in the hole in a better way and become a better competitor, this course is for you.

You may be a parent of a competitive junior athlete saying, "I wish I knew how to enhance my child's performance. I want to approach competitive athletics in a way that doesn't stress or divide the family, but enhances and builds the relationship." This course is for you, too. The last thing you want as a family is for the family to serve the sport. We want the sport to serve the family. *The Champion's Way* is an exceptional way to build your family through creating a common performance language.

This training works for a coach, too. You may be a coach of a team at a school or an organization, looking for a way to develop character, champion mindsets, and motivation for excellence. This is a great system for your team, as it focuses on the foundations of peak performance.

You may be an adult competitor who is wondering, "I'm past my prime, but I still have something inside of me. I have a championship I want to go for. I want to enhance my peak performance in my competition." This is a great system for you to see how to weave peak performance into your life, your business, and your family in a holistic way. Actually, this is an excellent program for anybody dedicated to achieving personal goals. It will lay the foundation for you from a personal growth approach.

It's also a great course if you're a student. I've taken many medical students through this process when they were about to take their big exam. I've had students fail, and they had to come back and retake the exam within six weeks. I take them through *The Champion's Way* process. They learn the dynamics and principles of peak performance. They pass their test with flying colors and achieve the results they desire.

I want to encourage you. Maybe you're an athlete, a coach, a business person, or someone with personal goals. If you hear a voice inside saying, "I want to release the champion within" and realize your full potential, *The Champion's Way* is for you. Let's get started!

MODULE 1 WORKSHEET

1. The two distinguishing features of champions are

   _____ and _____ .

2. My passion for golf began with my story on the putting green as a little girl. What story describes your passion for the game?

3. What story or experience most reflects superior focus for you?

4. On a scale of 1 to 10, with 1 being "none" and 10 being "outstanding," how would you rate yourself on the passion and focus scale right now?

   Passion 1 2 3 4 5 6 7 8 9 10

   Focus 1 2 3 4 5 6 7 8 9 10

5. What are the five core values of *The Champion's Way*?

   P _____

   R _____

   E _____

   W _____

   F _____

6. Which value are you the strongest in?

7. What value would you like to grow in and more strongly to reflect?

8. Is there another value that more accurately reflects wholeness to you?

9. Performance + _____ = wholeness

10. If you played your competitive season from a place of wholeness, what would you need to add to your life? Your game? What would you need to subtract from your life? Your game?

11. As an individual or as a team, create your own equation of 5 factors or values that you can OWN and LIVE out this season that reflects wholeness for you:

_____ + _____ +

_____ + _____ +

_____ = Wholeness.

12. Why is wholeness important?

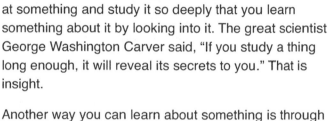

THE CHAMPION'S WAY

MODULE 2

How Peak Performance Happens: My Story

There are many different ways that you can learn something. Actually, I think there are three specific ways. One is through insight— being able to look at something and study it so deeply that you learn something about it by looking into it. The great scientist George Washington Carver said, "If you study a thing long enough, it will reveal its secrets to you." That is insight.

Another way you can learn about something is through foresight. As a competitive golfer, whenever I was preparing for a championship, I would learn the golf course. How do you learn it? You learn it from the tee forward all the way to the green. You are looking forward at something that's ahead of you. That's foresight.

There's a third way to learn something; it's hindsight. You learn by looking back at something and observing what you see. When I leave a hole and look back on it, I can learn so much about that hole that I couldn't see by looking forward at it. Many times, by looking back on a hole, you can see a lot more slope to the fairway than you can by looking at it from the tee. You can also see in a different way where the hazards are located, simply by looking back on them.

How does that relate to learning about peak performance? I want to begin this training by sharing with you a story from my own personal journey of my first major championship and what I learned about peak performance by looking back at it; that is, from hindsight.

In this training, we will begin to define the components of peak performance. We want to be able to take apart the pieces, look at a performance, and say, "This is how we got the result that we did." Any good competitor and any good coach must to be able to examine and know the components of peak performance.

The story of my first major championship didn't start from success, but from failure. Everything I learned from this experience set up my lifelong journey of seeking to discover all the dynamics that create a winning result, not just the ones that are obvious. My foundational story also set up my lifelong quest to answer the question: "How do I go about being a competitor and push my limits to achieve peak performance in a way that promotes and enhances my life instead of destroying it?" Finally, it set up my whole coaching philosophy and training on *The Champion's Way*, as I unpacked the treasures of knowledge and wisdom I gained through hindsight.

Assignment

Here is an assignment for you. As I share this story, begin to make a list of all the components of performance that you can identify—whatever attitude, skillset, mindset, or attribute that goes into the story. Write down as many factors as you can determine. (You can use the worksheet at the end of the chapter to do this assignment.)

My First Championship Story

When I was a teenager, I started to compete seriously in regional competition. One summer, when I was eighteen, I had a defining competitive moment that impacted me for life.

That summer, it seemed that if anybody beat me in a competition in junior tournaments, it was always one girl and by one shot. Her name was Nancy Rubin. We were friends off the course, but on the course, we were fierce competitors.

We had just completed a tournament where I lost again. I believed that I had just as much skill and ability as Nancy, and was passionately determined that I was finally going to beat her.

Our next match was the West Penn Junior Championship, and I was dead set on winning. It was match play, which means we played hole-by-hole versus aggregate score.

We completed eighteen holes of grueling match play, and we were even. We had to go to sudden death, which means we started off at the first hole again. I hit my shot right down the fairway. She hit her shot over in the rough. I thought, "I'm finally going to win this hole to claim the championship."

I got on the green in two shots. Her second shot landed in the trap. She hit on, a good distance from the hole. I got down in two putts for a par 4. She had to snake in a twenty-five footer to tie me. I thought, "There's no way she's going to do that after coming out of a trap." To my surprise, she confidently stepped up to her putt and hit it right in the hole to tie me with a par.

We got to the next hole, a par 5. I hit my shot down the fairway. For a split second, I let up on my concentration. My second shot faded to the right and settled under the trees. An official came out about a half hour later and deemed my ball OB, out of bounds. It was a horrendous hole. I ended up with a double bogey, a seven. She scored a five. I lost again to Nancy Rubin.

The next week was the West Penn Amateur, the most prestigious tournament in Western Pennsylvania. It's not a junior tournament, but the big amateur championship of the year.

I was determined that if I got pitted against Nancy Rubin again, I was going to win. I kept announcing to myself: "I don't care if she has a three, I'm going to have a two. If she has a two, I'm going to have a one. If she has a one, I'll find a way to make a zero, but I am not going to lose again." I set my mind. It was amazing how I ate, slept, drank, and totally put myself in the energy of the win before I ever got there.

I advanced to the semifinals. Guess who I had to play? Nancy Rubin. We got through eighteen holes, even. Nineteen holes, even. Twenty holes, even. Twenty-one holes, even. The twenty-second hole was a par 3. I hit my shot on the green. She missed her shot in the rough. She ended up with a four, a bogey. All I had to do was two-putt from forty feet to finally beat Nancy Rubin.

I took a good look at my first putt, put a nice stroke on it, and hit it about four feet from the cup. All I had between me and my win was a four-foot- putt. It broke a little left-to-right. I must have stared at that hole for what seemed like eternity, thinking it might just expand.

I finally hit my putt, and it rolled toward the hole. Then it turned slightly to the right . . . and dropped in. Yeah! I finally beat Nancy Rubin! It was an amazing match. I felt like I'd won the whole West Penn Amateur Championship! It was a huge personal victory for me.

The only problem was, I still had to play the finals the next day against the seventh-ranked amateur in the United States.

Now, I'm the pipsqueak from the other side of the tracks. Here I was playing this well-accomplished, highly successful, jet-set millionaire who was the seventh-ranked amateur in the United States. I wasn't thinking about her. It never entered my mind that I would be in a position to win the entire championship. Psychologically and emotionally, my goal had been to gain my personal victory of beating Nancy. But now what?

The next day, while on the first tee, I thought, "How does my mindset change? How do I think differently? What am I to do now?" I remember getting a little note from the pro at the course. When he handed it to me, I saw that it was from my swing coach who wrote, "You've worked hard. This is your time. Go win that thing!"

I reflected again. "I just beat Nancy Rubin, which was my goal, and now I'm playing in the finals. What is my mindset? I've never played a seventh-ranked amateur in the United States before, so I'll just do what I can. I'll do my best."

We were both playing great golf. We got to the fourteenth hole, and I was one up on the seventh-ranked amateur in the United States. She proceeded to hit her drive out of bounds. She then sent her next drive into the sand trap, which further enhanced my lead.

I stepped up and hit my drive off the fairway, a little behind a bunker, but no big deal. It was a par 4, and all I needed to do was get a five on the hole. She was going to make at least a six. I could easily win the hole and go on to put myself in a strong position to win the championship. However, it never entered my mind that a bogey would win the hole.

In taking my shot, I didn't ask my caddy for his advice. I pulled out a wood when I only needed an iron. I proceeded to hit the freakiest shot I have ever hit in my life. My 3-wood-shot hit the edge of the sand trap right in front of me (that I wasn't even in). The ball took a reverse "L" flight and landed in the woods. The official came out a half hour later and deemed my ball out-of-bounds. It was a déjà vu of the week before with Nancy.

We'd had numerous birdies throughout the day, but this hole was a disaster. While I was walking toward the hole, my opponent said to me, "You're on in seven, and I'm on in six."

I thought, "What? That's not true."

There were all kinds of spectators watching what was going on. I knew I had to accurately assess my score. I thought, "One, two, three . . ." I nervously recounted my score.

A second time she exclaimed, "You're on in seven, and I'm on in six."

All of a sudden I started to feel the pressure. I recounted my shots again. "One, two, three—no!" A third time my opponent looked at me and said, "You're on in seven, and I'm on in six!" With a crowd all around me and the pressure mounting, I didn't know what to do.

I had to make a decision. Right in the middle of the battle, I had to determine what was real. Here's my exact thought: "She must know what she's talking about. She's more experienced than I am."

We got to the hole and conceded putts. When you concede to losing a hole, the winner gets the honor of teeing up first on the next hole in match play. She stepped up to tee off first. Everybody was looking around saying, "Why is she teeing off first?"

I responded, "She won the hole."

They said, "Oh no, she didn't. You were both on in the same number of strokes." Because I conceded to losing the hole, I lost. We both birdied the fifteenth hole. She went on to win the tournament by a narrow margin.

I was devastated. I lost when I could have won. I lost when I should have won. My loss had absolutely nothing to do with the fact that I wasn't in a position to win or didn't have the skill to win, or that I didn't have a desire to win. I lost because of how I saw myself. I put more confidence in who my opponent was than in myself. As a result, I put more confidence in her voice than in my own.

My caddy later said to me, "Veronica, if you had just asked me what club to hit, I never would have told you to take that three-wood. I would have told you to take an iron, lay up, and get your bogey, but you didn't ask me."

Later on, I talked to the official about it. She said, "If you had just come over and asked me what the score was, I could have stepped in to help out." I didn't even know that I could approach her with that question. It was the first time I'd been in that kind of situation.

I lost for reasons that had nothing to do with my skill. They had to do with relational reasons. The first reason was how I saw myself. I saw myself as a winner with Nancy, but I did not see myself as a winner during the final match. I thought more highly of my opponent than I thought of myself.

That one relational dynamic underlies the groundwork of *The Champion's Way* approach to peak performance. It's that winning, competing, and the whole idea of peak performance doesn't begin with something "out there." It begins with something "inside of you." It has to do with how you see yourself. You have to begin to see yourself as a champion, because your identity determines the road map to everything else.

When I got home that afternoon, I was upset and felt totally devastated. My mom was lying on the bed crying. They had broadcasted the entire championship on the radio. In that moment, I so desperately needed somebody to hold me, to hug me, to let me know that everything was all right. I needed to hear that I was loved, regardless of my losing the championship.

Unfortunately, my mom was so distraught that I ended up consoling her, instead of her being able to console me. As a result, I received no consolation for my squandered victory. Not knowing how to process the letdown of my competition, I buried my emotions and defeat. The impact of that loss affected me so deeply that I completely forgot to enter the championship the following year.

I share my story with you because within it we can unpack all the components of peak performance. We will talk about them and define them. These elements will help you start from a very intentional place of success on your road to championship.

It was in hindsight that I learned about the how's and why's of my loss. I wish I'd had a performance coach at that time to help me process my defeat, but I didn't. However, as a performance coach who helps others like you think like a champion, I'm going to help you set up for success from the start. I'm going to help you get really clear and knowledgeable about how to put yourself in the best position possible to win. I'm going to instill in you "1st tee champion mindset thinking," so you can avoid the 14th tee defeat when faced with making decisions under pressure. It all begins with understanding how performance happens. It begins with seeing yourself as a champion before all else. It begins with the win from within.

Let's take a deeper look into this story to discover the components of peak performance.

MODULE 2 WORKSHEET

1. The 3 ways you can learn something are through:

    a._____

    b._____

    c._____

2. Give an example of when you experienced each kind of learning.

3. What is your reaction to the story of my losing my first big championship?

4. List all the components of performance that you identified from my West
Penn Amateur story:

_____   _____

_____   _____

_____   _____

_____   _____

_____   _____

_____   _____

5. Can you identify categories within your list of components?

THE CHAMPION'S WAY

MODULE 3

Discover the Power of Process-Oriented Goals: The Four Champion Zones

That was part of the story of my first major championship at the West Penn Amateur, and how I lost when I could have won.

I gave you an assignment. In it, I wanted you to list as many different components, attributes, and ingredients to the competition as you could. When I've done this with many students, here are some of the answers that they give: concentration, focus, determination, skill, desire, practice. What else? Instruction, learning, physical fitness, fear, confidence. You could go on and list all the things that comprise a performance, which really have to do with much more than just the physical mechanics of your swing, whatever sport that you're in.

I could further list many more attributes and components than this, but actually, when you take all the different facets of what makes up a performance, it boils down to four major categories. I want to define what those categories are, because everything that we listed can fall into one of them. These categories make up the components of performance Champion Zones:

1. Physical

2. Mental

3. Emotional

4. Spiritual

To achieve a peak performance, you must be fully engaged in each of the four champion zones concurrently. This is the *The Champion's Way*. What does it mean to be fully engaged? Dr. James Loehr, a world-renowned peak performance trainer, says it best: "To be fully engaged is to be physically energized, mentally focused, emotionally connected, and spiritually aligned." All of those things have to be working together to achieve a peak performance. When you can define a process in each one of the champion zones, and then do them all together at the same time, that's when you take a leap in your performance.

Why is this so incredible? Most people, particularly if they're at the beginning of their competitive journey, look only at the result. "I didn't get a peak performance. I shot 95 instead of 75." Then you go back and just try to work harder. You don't understand the different parts that come into that unless you can look back on your performance and say, "Was that high score a result of what happened in the physical zone? Was it emotional? Was it mental or was it spiritual?"

I can remember playing many years ago with a PGA pro named Chip Beck. Chip was one of the players who shot a 59. It was one of the rare, amazing performances of a golf professional. One day after he was playing, Chip said he went back and analyzed his round. He said, "I only had three mental errors today." I was already a golf professional, but I'd never heard of someone going back and examining his mental errors. All I was thinking about was the physical zone; namely, my swing mechanics. Chances are, if you're in your teenage years and a competitive junior athlete, most of the time you'll hang out in the physical zone.

However, we all experience emotions. We all experience concentration or the lack of it. We all have a sense of mission or meaning, or we don't. So, now let's define each of these categories and set up a process you can engage in to help you be fully immersed in each zone to achieve maximum progress and results.

What makes up each zone? I will define them and then give you an example of a true champion student who put it all together for a peak performance.

The Physical Zone

The physical zone entails fitness, nutrition, swing mechanics, and energy management.

In recent years, physical fitness has become just as important as swing mechanics—the physical aspects of your swing in whatever sport you're engaged in. Fitness has many different components to it: strength, flexibility, endurance, speed, balance, and power. Many sports now have sport-specific trainers where you can learn the functional aspects of your swing movements and improve your swing in the gym. The bottom line is, you want to make sure you are strong in each aspect of physical fitness and that you understand how proper fitness helps empower you in your sport.

If you're a young person on the front end of your journey, I've found that it's highly important to work on endurance. Many junior players don't get enough hydration or eat enough during a round. As a result, their endurance is cut short. Frequently, a younger player will practice up until the very last moment of starting a competition. They become tired, and consequently sabotage their strength.

If you're at the more senior level of your competitive journey, it's most important to work on your recovery or energy management.

For instance, when I go to play in a tournament now, I'm very conscious of my energy, because you never want to go into a competition from a tired place. Champions perform from a place of rest. Now, I'll go in a day early. I will do my practice round, and I'll have a day of rest before the tournament starts, because it takes a senior player longer to recover her energy. That's energy management.

You may be interested in gaining more strength if you're a social player and don't have a lot of strength. Many women who are beginners and want to move from being a social golfer to a competitive golfer have to be able to hit the ball farther. They have got to get stronger. All the elements of fitness come in, as well as flexibility, the older you get. You can pick out one aspect of physical fitness and make that your process: fitness, nutrition, swing mechanics, and energy management.

I've worked with many students, particularly grad students, who are studying really hard for a major exam. It's amazing how smart they are about their studies, but how "dumb" they are with regard to how they prepare to take an exam. Often students will say to me, "I lose concentration in the middle of the morning, and I can't even think straight." Do you know the first thing I do? I ask them, "What did you have for breakfast?" Without fail, someone will say, "I drink two glasses of orange juice." I say, "No wonder you can't think mid-morning. Your blood sugar has dipped to a level where you can't think."

It's extremely important when you're going for a peak performance— whether it's a tournament, a competition, a test—that you are very clear and strong about the physical fitness aspect of your game. This also means getting enough sleep.

Once I did a study of a group of freshmen high school students. I asked them, "What is the average amount of sleep that you get?" Do know what the average was? Five hours. I said, "How can your brain think with only five hours of sleep?" You want to be careful and clear about your processes in the physical arena: your fitness, your nutrition, your swing mechanics, and your energy management.

Regarding swing mechanics, it's essential to find the right coach. I know a lot of times you think you can do something on your own, or maybe you're a parent coaching your child and you think, "I've got this covered," but having the right coach makes all the difference in the world. Recently, my game opened up to a whole new place after I found the right coach who actually fixed a part of my swing that I'd been wanting to improve for decades. I had gone to many fine teachers, but I found the right coach, and what a difference it made!

Fitness, nutrition, swing mechanics, and energy management: miss out on one of the elements, and your peak performance will suffer. Be sure to work on all of them at the same time, and you will succeed along the road to championship!

The Mental Zone

The second zone—the mental zone—is comprised of focus, concentration, and champion mindsets. Do you know that champions think differently than other people? They think a certain way, called mindsets. When you learn these mindsets, you will go up in your "champ-o-meter." We're going to talk about what some of those mindsets are. I have dedicated a whole module on champion mindsets.

Focus and concentration are elements of mental toughness. Mental toughness is your ability to direct your mind to a target and sustain a thought long enough to where you can execute it, and then execute those shots under pressure. It's really important to develop mental toughness. We're going to talk about how to do that, because this attribute is so important in the whole area of developing peak performance.

In your champion development, you want to grow in your ability to get in the zone intentionally through becoming strong in the mental zone.

The Emotional Zone

The third zone is called the emotional zone. All people experience emotions, but when it comes to mastering their emotions, there's a shortage of knowledge. Champions have emotional mastery, so we're going talk about a grid for emotions that basically falls into two categories: empowering and disempowering emotions.

We all have a most empowering emotion and a most disempowering emotion. When you can identify each one, you can more intentionally go to the empowering one and avoid the disempowering one. This is important because the emotional zone has so much to do with your getting into the flow of performance.

The Spiritual Zone

The fourth zone is the most undefined zone for most people. Some peak performance coaches don't even believe there is a spiritual component to performance, but I do because the spiritual zone has to do with the essence of who you are. The physical has to do with your body, the mental has to do with your mind, but the spiritual has to do with your spirit, the essence of who you are as a person.

In performance, I define the spiritual zone in three different categories. One is identity, how you see yourself. In my story of the West Penn Amateur, I saw myself as a winner with Nancy Rubin, but I didn't see myself as a winner with the seventh-ranked amateur in the United States. You could see how that played such a major role in the outcome of my performance. Identity is indeed a key piece in achieving peak performance.

The second is higher purpose. Why do you play your sport? If you can determine a larger purpose in your sport, with any achievement you'll have a greater sense of motivation and determination. Regardless of the outcome, it will have meaning to you. So much of the reason why we don't have a peak performance is because we attach too much meaning to the score. In *The Champion's Way*, we want to attach meaning to something outside the score, so that regardless of those numbers, you can function from a more centered and stable place.

Therefore, we always want competition—whether it's in sports, business, academics, or just some personal goals—to serve the larger purpose of your life. You always want to have a higher purpose for your play. Why are you doing what you're doing?

The third element to the spiritual zone is your values. We want to establish inner values. For me, one of those is integrity. Do I conduct myself in a way that is as consistent on the outside as it is on the inside? Part of that is calling myself up higher and living from my highest self. Another part of that is to love myself while I'm going through my sport, and to inspire others as I go about my competition. You want to develop a set of values that will help determine your decisions and the path that you take, so that the score won't have dominance over you. Instead, you're going to stand in your own space, call your own shots, and perform from the inside-out place that we've been talking about.

In review, students of *The Champion's Way* function from a place of being fully engaged to achieve peak performance.

Champion's Way students also shift from result-oriented goals to process-oriented goals when they focus on operating in the four champion zones. What is a process? Let's say I want to finish in the top ten in a tournament. I'm not going to focus on just the result and on working harder to get there. Instead, I'm going to go back and say, "What is the process in the physical zone that I need to accomplish in order to get to my goal? How will I have to think? What will my emotional state need to be, and why am I doing this?"

If we can define the processes—what you do on your way to the goal—and do those things concurrently, you're going to set yourself up to get the score. That's what a process-oriented goal is.

Example

I want to give you an example of a student who went through the Champion Zones and created success from the start. She utilized the Champion Zone sheet which you can find at the end of this module. Most of your involvement in applying *The Champion's Way* will boil down to working with the Champion Zone sheet. (See Appendix A.)

Many years ago I met a young golfer who was playing in the U.S. Kids World Championship. Her name was Lexi. It was her first major world championship. I met her and her father in Pinehurst, North Carolina, and we got to talking.

I mentioned to her, "This is your first championship. How do you feel? Are you excited?"

She replied, "I'm afraid. I'm a bit nervous."

I said, "What are you a bit nervous about?"

She said, "I'm not sure how I'm going to deal with a bad shot."

"You know you are going to have a bad shot, don't you? What if we could go into this championship not focused from the start on what you think your outcome is going to be, but why don't we go into this championship creating success from the start? You're going to define, from a process-oriented base, what success looks like on the front end."

We went through the four zones. All of the processes came out of a conversation with Lexi. I asked her some powerful questions to bring out what was inside of her. I engaged her father only when it was necessary to amplify her answers. Asking powerful questions is the key to discovering what is inside of someone. That's the only way to determine what their processes are, as *The Champion's Way* is an inside-out approach.

I asked her, "Do you have a feel for the greens?"

"No."

I said, "A feel for the greens is the most important thing you need if you're playing in a tournament. If you have nothing else, you need a feel for the greens, which is knowing how hard or how soft to hit a putt." We went over to the putting green and I gave her feel drills to work on so she would gain confidence in her putting.

Behind every process is a practice. The first thing we did in the physical zone was to give her the process of having a feel for the greens. Then we created practices that would support that process.

Then I focused on the mental zone. I asked, "How are you going to deal with a bad shot?"

"I don't know," she answered.

I said, "What do you do when a mosquito lands on your shoulder?"

She smiled while she flicked the imaginary mosquito off her shoulder.

"Let's add some language to that."

"Bye-bye," she replied. Her father looked at her and smiled.

I said, "This is great, because now we're creating a common language so that when your father caddies for you, he doesn't have to stay silent, or he doesn't have to worry that he's going to upset you. If he sees you hanging on to a bad shot, do you give him permission to look at you and say, 'Bye-bye'?"

"Yes." They both smiled.

The way she determined from the start that she was going to deal with a bad shot was to flick it off so the battle stayed on the outside. We came up with, "Flick off bad shot," as a mental toughness process.

For dealing with the emotional zone, I asked, "What kind of emotional state do you want to characterize your play?" She said, "I want to be free." We talked through her desired emotional state more fully to also include enjoying herself and to let go of the need to control the outcome so she could enjoy her time. We called her emotional zone "free," to denote being fearless and free.

For the last one, the spiritual zone, I asked her, "What is your higher purpose for playing this week? You came all the way from Wisconsin. If anything, this is a week where you should also leave with a memory. Regardless of how you play, your dad's here. He's going to caddy for you. I think you should leave with at least a good memory. What is a higher purpose for playing?"

She said, "To have fun with my dad."

I replied, "Great."

There we have it. Now she had four processes, and we boiled each one down to four words: feel, flick, free, and fun. We called them the four "F's." She wrote them down on a 3-by-5 index card and plastered them everywhere she went. She put a card on the cart where she could see it. and looked at it after every hole.

After the first day her father ran up to me and said, "Lexi had a ten. Did she ever handle it great! She flicked that thing off, and I was so proud of her!"

Now what would have happened if they hadn't created that process from the start? That ten could have been a real failure, but she had a process. Because of the way she responded to that poor performance, she actually had a victory.

After the third day, the father came up to me and exclaimed, "My daughter just had the best competitive round of her life. She had a 77 in her first world championship and we had the best time we ever had as a father and daughter on the golf course. We can't wait to come back next year."

They created success from the start, and they ended up having a peak performance. She was able to take home her Champion Zone processes and build on them for the next year. That's *The Champion's Way* of being fully engaged: physically energized, mentally focused, emotionally connected, and spiritually aligned. She played from a place of relationship with herself and her father. That's true personal power.

I want to refer back to my West Penn Amateur Championship. Had I known *The Champion's Way* going into my first championship, it would have been a very different outcome. I would have known how to process my experience. However, I didn't have a process-oriented way of looking at competition. I didn't know how to process my performance. I didn't know how to shift my strategy. I didn't know how to continue my focus on that last round. From my failure, I gained all this learning that I'm going to impart to you. I'm going to

The Champion's Way

help you so you'll be on a continuum of growth and advancement on the road to championship.

The Champion Zones - Defining Your Process-oriented Goals

Physical — swing mechanics/fitness/nutrition/energy management

1   2   3   4   5   6   7   8   9   10

Mental — focus/concentration/champion mindsets

1   2   3   4   5   6   7   8   9   10

Emotional — empowering vs. disempowering emotions

1   2   3   4   5   6   7   8   9   10

Spiritual — identity/ values/higher purpose

1   2   3   4   5   6   7   8   9   10

My champion challenge/championship is:

MODULE 3 WORKSHEET

1. The four categories of performance are as follows:

   P _____

   M _____

   E _____

   S _____

2. According to world renowned trainer Dr. James Loehr, peak performance happens from a place of being fully engaged. To be fully engaged is to be:

   Physically _____

   Mentally _____   _____

   Emotionally _____

   Spiritually _____   _____

3. The physical zone is comprised of: Swing mechanics, Fitness,

   _____ and _____.

4. The mental zone is made up of:_____,

   Concentration and Champion Mindsets, Champions think

   _____ than other people.

5. The emotional zone is made up of empowering and
    _____ emotions.

6. What is your most disempowering emotion? _____.

    Most empowering one? _____.

7. The spiritual zone is comprised of: _____,
    _____, and _____.

8. What zone do you focus on the most?

9. What zone are you the most unfamiliar with?

10. What could you accomplish if you had clarity and full engagement in all
    four zones at the same time?

11. Can you remember a time when you did? Describe your experience of
    being fully engaged:

12. To what extent do you believe you can intentionally create "being in the
    zone"?

13. What does creating success from the start mean?

14. What is the difference between a results-oriented goal and a process-oriented goal?

15. What processes do you need to work on to advance to the next level? Identify one process in each zone:

Physically _____

Mentally _____

Emotionally _____

Spiritually ____ _____

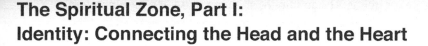

THE CHAMPION'S WAY

MODULE 4

The Spiritual Zone, Part I:
Identity: Connecting the Head and the Heart

In these next modules, I'm going to define each champion zone more specifically. I will share with you some concrete examples of how to work out the process and the practice behind each one. The goal in this training is for you to experience a peak performance and be able to put all the processes together. As much as this book is an educational training, education alone isn't going to bring you a result. We must combine education with application to have a transformation.

It's important for you to begin to shift the way you look at peak performance from something that's merely results-driven and outward-to-in, to being inward-to-out.

In this module, we will dive into the spiritual zone, which is identity, higher purpose, and values.

Many years ago, I started explaining *The Champion's Way* with the physical zone, but because this is an inside-out process, I now always begin with the spiritual. The spiritual zone has to do with how you see yourself as a champion, and to define "champion" based on a place of identity, not just results.

I remember talking to the great Peggy Kirk Bell one day. She was one of the founding members of the LPGA, and a great lady golfer. Some even call her the Arnold Palmer of women's golf. "Mrs. Bell," I said, "What's a champion?" "Someone who wins," was her response.

A champion is a winner, but not all winners are champions. We want you to begin to understand that being a champion isn't so much about a trophy you achieve but an identity you walk out and realize daily. It's how you live your life.

Let me give you a couple of examples of some budding champions and how they came to develop confidence in their inner knowing, that inner acceptance of who they are.

The first one is a girl named Meghan. When Meghan came to me, she was a competitive junior golfer. At age fifteen, she was already a high academic achiever who saw herself as a champion, having all the practices and the processes of being a great student.

Unfortunately, in golf she lacked confidence on the first tee. In fact, when she teed off in a tournament, she imploded. She defined herself based on peer pressure—what everybody else was thinking about her—and crumbled within. Of course, no one was really thinking anything about her. But if you're a teenager in your own personal formation, it's typical for you to define who you are based on how you think everybody else sees you. In her mindset, her approach was still outside-in.

In her first coaching session, we immediately began to define her processes. Since she was already a champion student, I began from where she already had complete confidence. I asked her, "When you turn in a paper or an assignment, are you thinking about what anybody else thinks about that?"

She responded, "No, that's ridiculous."

"Are you fearful of how others might criticize you or see you and your paper or finished assignment?"

"No, that's ridiculous."

"So," I replied, "you already have a champion process and a champion identity in your academics?"

"Yeah," she said.

"Then guess what? The same processes in academics work for athletics. If you already see yourself as an academic champion, all we need to do is transfer those same processes over to athletics and begin to pull on that identity that you already have as a champion."

We worked hard on making her inner-champion identity in academics a transferable truth to her golf. I gave her certain assignments in her practices as a golfer that we would grade. I told her, "Your first assignment is to make an A in your practice session and do it with the same excellence, the same diligence, the same kind of strategic methodology that you have in your academics." We came from a place that she could already identify with and then began to transfer that. It was an effective and beautiful process that worked in her mental zone.

Regarding the spiritual zone, I told her, "We're going to create some declarations. A declaration is a practice that connects your head and heart together so there's no disparity between what you think you'd like to achieve and your sense of inner confidence, and knowing that you can achieve it. If we can connect the head and heart through declarations, which is the affirmation of who you are, then you will begin to create a great inner confidence and strength in the inner core of your champion identity."

Then I said, "I want you to write down twenty-five reasons why you believe you should be in the champion's circle."

Here are some of her answers, which she titled: "Reasons Why I Have What It Takes to Win."

- I have a lot of passion for golf, for my sport.
- I love to practice, and I'm up on my game.
- I have a great attitude about the game
- I enjoy playing the game.
- I've grown to enjoy competition.
- I finished second in my regional tournament and third in another tournament, and I'm gaining momentum.
- I have a great coach and great teammates.
- I have a higher purpose for playing.
- I really like the course.
- I'm in good health.

- I believe in myself.
- I can achieve anything I set my mind to.
- Why not me?

Here's the one that stood out above and beyond all the rest: "I have everything inside of me I need to be to be the champion I desire to be." We edited it to say, "I have everything I need to be the champion I desire to be."

She listed others:

- I look good.
- My dad believes in me.
- I've got a good set of skills.
- I'm working on specific shots.

I asked her, "Of those, what are the top five truths in your list?" She went through and checked off the top five. I continued, "Check off the top three," and then, "Check off the top one." Her number one statement that was most true for her was: "I have everything I need to be the champion I desire to be."

Then I said, "On a scale of 1 to 10 with 1 being, 'This is untrue,' to 10 being, 'This is totally true,' how strong of a personal truth is that to you?"

She replied, "It's a 10."

I said, "That's the centerpiece of your identity. It is your main declaration." She put the declaration on a card, and for the next three weeks she plastered that truth inside her head and her heart. She declared it out loud several times a day. She got really centered on her inner belief and knowing.

 She came to me shooting 88. I worked with her diligently during the three weeks before the state championship. She participated in the championship shooting the best round of her life, which was also the best competitive score of her life. She shot a 76, and her focus was amazing. She finished third in the state championship!

Instead of being defined from the outside in, she began to define herself from the inside out. I often say to someone at the beginning stage of their formation, "It's totally typical for a fifteen-year-old to wonder what everybody else is thinking about them. However, do you want to be a typical teenager, or do you want to be a champion?"

They will say, "Oh, I want to be a champion."

"Then we have to think like a champion, and a champion defines herself. A champion speaks from her own voice."

Referring to my own teenage experience, I put more trust in my opponent's voice in the West Penn Amateur than in my own voice. If you are a competitive athlete, I encourage you to write down twenty-five declarations, twenty-five statements that are true of you. Pick the top five, then pick the top one, and declare it out loud. Look at yourself in the mirror. You've got to state it, not just read it. You have to put sound to it to allow that identity piece to really be strengthened in you.

I want to give you another example of someone who found victory through engaging the spiritual zone. In this case, the concept of higher purpose is highlighted.

Alyssa came to me from Canada. She was playing in the U.S. Kids World Championship. I asked her, "What is your goal in this tournament?"

She said, "I'd like to finish in the top ten."

I went through all the process-oriented zones with Alyssa and found out she was already a champion. She had already won, and thought of herself in the highest way.

However, when we did a deep-dive conversation in the physical zone, we discovered that she lacked endurance. She petered out after hole 16, lacking the energy she needed to play an entire eighteen holes.

Mentally, she was already focused, but only for sixteen holes. Emotionally, she was engaged and passionate about her game. Because she lacked endurance and focus for the last two holes, she also lost concentration as well. We really needed her to refocus so that she could be mentally dialed in for an entire eighteen holes.

I persuaded her to drink more water and eat more food bars to help with energy levels. Things began to click when I addressed the spiritual zone. I asked, "What is your higher purpose for playing?"

She responded, "No one's ever asked me that question before."

I said, "Many times a higher purpose is to play in honor of somebody."

She paused for a minute, then said, "My grandmother has cancer. I'm going to do birdies for Grandma!"

"That's wonderful!" I exclaimed.

She went out and got a big chart. Any birdies she scored, she would record them on the chart. When the tournament was done, the chart would become a card she would present to her grandma.

Because we were in the process of becoming fully engaged, once I defined her processes, we could put it all together. I told her, "I want you to do something very special on holes 17 and 18. I want you to particularly dedicate those holes to birdies for Grandma." This became her higher purpose to re-engage herself mentally.

She played great. On the last two days, she birdied holes 17 and 18, fully engaged in her higher purpose of scoring birdies for Grandma. She was mentally focused and had endurance for the entire 18 holes as she implemented all four champion zones.

 Alyssa finished sixth in the world championship doing birdies for Grandma! Three years later, she qualified for the Canadian Women's Open at age thirteen. Her grandfather died that week, but instead of being emotionally devastated, disconnected, and disengaged, she did birdies for Grandpa. She finished in the top fifty in the Canadian Women's Open at only thirteen years of age, and during a time when her grandfather had passed!

I learned that the champion spirit was still inside her three years after I'd coached her. It was a beautiful, internalized truth for her. Alyssa was a true champion, doing *The Champion's Way* of being physically energized, mentally focused, emotionally connected, and spiritually aligned. Her golf took on incredible meaning as she engaged in the spiritual principle of playing in honor of a loved one.

Sue was another young competitor who began to work on the spiritual zone. She experienced an amazing breakthrough when she released her inner champion identity.

When Sue came to me, she was shooting around 85. When she shot a poor score, she would lose it to the point where she cried for the rest of the round. A poor shot would totally devastate her. While her breakdown was in the emotional zone, what she really needed was to strengthen the core of her inner champion to make her spirit stronger than her emotions. We crafted some major declarations. Sue had the ability to be very determined when she wanted to be, but she was allowing the outside-in approach to weaken her. Our aim was to shift her thinking and play inside out, starting with her champion identity.

Here are some of the declarations that Sue created:

- I am a totally confident player.
- I step up to each shot from the place of calm concentration.
- I am an expert at using my mental triggers where I slash, kill, execute, and demean all negative, intruding thoughts with glee.
- I consider all thoughts of fear, inadequacy, and self-pity to be my enemies.
- I have total victory over all my mental, emotional, and spiritual enemies because I am victorious, and I am a champion.
- Watch out, world, here I come! I am a fierce competitor.
- I put my game face on, from the first tee all the way through to the final shot.
- My scores must improve because I'm playing from a place of victory.
- With these powerful declarations, I have a feeling of power and confidence I've never known before.

When Sue got hold of her declarations and they became part of her inner truth, she busted loose at the very next tournament. She went from shooting around 85 to 74. She led the tournament the first day. Her 74 was the best round of her life. She played from the spiritual zone of engaging her champion identity. Her greatness was unleashed when she connected her head and her heart.

I want to finish this module by giving you an example that's not athletic, but from business.

I've coached many people going through a career transition who come to me when they have an interview scheduled with a company and want to put their best foot forward. But when they talk to me about the person who will be interviewing them, they often come in from a place of fear, wondering, "Will I measure up to the company's expectation? How will they see me?"

I immediately flip it. I say, "I want you to go into that interview from a place of total confidence in who you are. If for some reason who you are doesn't line up with the person they're looking for, it's not a matter of your looking for their approval. It's a matter of your going in and saying, 'Hey, this is who I am. I'm coming from a place of confidence from the center of who I am.' Then you can go in from a place of peace and confidence, self-worth, and esteem." I go through the same process with executives, so that they go into the interview process from a place of centeredness and true identity. Then they can process that from a place of peace versus a place of looking for outside approval. Their interview approach becomes a matter of alignment and congruence, not one of seeking approval.

Are you ready to join Meghan, Alyssa, and Sue in the spiritual champion zone? The following worksheet will help you to define your declarations. It's time to release your inner champion!

MODULE 4 WORKSHEET

The Champion's Way is an inside-out approach to peak performance. The innermost factor contributing to your performance is your IDENTITY. How you see yourself is causal to everything else. It's the lead domino, not your perfect swing mechanics. You cannot perform beyond how you SEE YOURSELF.

The Champion's Way approach is that being a champion is not based on a trophy you achieve, but on an IDENTITY you realize and walk out daily. It's WHO YOU ARE in your everyday life. It's how you live and how you see yourself.

Tapping into this reality begins by making declarations. Declarations connect your head and your heart so you are integrated as a person. Let's begin to create some declarations. These are statements that you believe to be true about you. Declarations begin with "I am . . ." or "I believe . . . "

Write down 25 reasons why you believe you deserve to be in the champions' circle:

1. _____

2. _____

3. _____

4. _____

5. _____

6. _____

7. _____

8. _____

9. _____

10. _____

11. _____

12. _____

13. _____

14. _____

15. _____

16. _____

17. _____

18. _____

19. _____

20. _____

21. _____

22. _____

23. _____

24. _____

25. _____

Circle the top five reasons that are most true to you.

Circle the top three that are most true to you.

Now circle the top one – the No. 1 statement that is most true about you.

That is the core of who you are in your belief system.

To drill home your belief, take a few 3-by-5 index cards and write down your most core belief on each. Put a card on your desk, on your mirror, your fridge—all the places it will be visible. Meditate on it several times a day. Get it down in your heart and up in your head at the same time. When you play out of who you are, you are playing as a true champion.

Declarations are the practice for creating a strong identity. Identity will create an inner confidence because you will step up to the tee to play FROM VICTORY, not to get victory. It doesn't matter how young or old you are. If you DEFINE who you are as a CHAMPION from the start, you are setting yourself up to create victory FROM THE START!

THE CHAMPION'S WAY

The Physical Zone: Developing Your Skillsets, Fitness, and Energy Management

The physical zone includes fitness, nutrition, swing mechanics, and energy management.

Many years ago, I was the mental game coach for a world-renowned junior golf academy. I was training twelve seventeen-year-old boys from Mexico. As you could probably imagine, given their age range and development, their major focus was in the physical zone. They loved to work out and practice their swings. They knew the importance of concentration and focus.

Many of them struggled with anger and other disempowering emotions. However, they were unaware of how to take charge of those emotions. Most also had never considered playing from a higher purpose or saw themselves as role models. It was quite a challenge for them to expand their focus to all four champion zones, not just the physical.

The physical zone is the one we're most familiar with and the easiest to define. It's an extremely important zone. Without the physical skill and capacity to do your sport, nothing else works. It's only through the physical zone of skill development that the other zones make any sense. In a way, then, it's the most important zone because it's foundational to your development.

Let's begin by exploring the elements of physical fitness.

The area of fitness is comprised of many different components. Among them are strength, flexibility, resilience, speed, endurance, balance, and power. You especially want to work on the strength part when you are young. Today's young players can enjoy the superior advancement of sport-specific fitness, which not only helps with overall fitness, but also with functional fitness for their sport.

In addition to physical fitness, I believe the most foundational element in the physical zone is the need for young people to get sound sleep. Champions perform from a place of rest. Earl Woods would always encourage Tiger to sleep in after a tournament for as long as twelve hours. He needed the physical recovery as much as he needed the physical workouts.

When you get older, you tend to have more issues with balance and flexibility. Often people fail to take the needed steps to make sure they have the range of motion required for playing their sport.

I was talking to three different men on the driving range one day. One had been a high-level competitor when he was in his twenties and thirties. Now that he was fifty, he started to have back problems. I told him, "If you want to continue to play at a high level in your fifties and beyond, you've got to work on your range of motion to make sure your back stays flexible and open. Do you do any kind of stretching? Do you do any kind of yoga?"

"No," he replied.

I encouraged him to do so. Look at Tiger Woods now. Because he swung so hard when he was young, he's had to deal with tremendous back problems as he's aged.

It's a real shame to have the skill and the desire to play but no longer the ability to do so because you don't have proper fitness. If the golfer I mentioned had learned *The Champion's Way*, he would have seen that doing things like yoga and stretching exercises would give him the physical ability to pursue his passion.

Another gentleman I met that day also loved golf. He was a bit older than the first man. However, he suffered from excruciating back pain to the point of being debilitated. I thought, "If he would only begin to care about his body as much as he cared about his passion, he would have a fighting chance. He could work on his range of motion and flexibility to make some shifts and changes. He could most likely pursue his sport without so much pain." In middle age and beyond, it's especially important to do what you need to do in the area of fitness so you can stay in the game.

The other part of the physical zone is nutrition. I always ask my students to define "what is causal" for them. In my case, I have to make sure my blood sugar level stays level. The moment my blood sugar goes down, I lose my focus, my stamina, and my concentration. While the physical mechanics of your game are important, factoring in how nutrition makes a difference is also key. One component affects the others.

The physical zone really made a difference with one of my true champion swimmers. Andrew came to me when he was about twelve years old. His mother shared with me that he had a dream of swimming in the state championship. She confessed that she didn't know how to release his potential. She wasn't sure if he even had the inner drive to compete.

In working with Andrew, the first thing I needed to determine was whether he had the physical fitness to achieve his goal and if he had a competitive spirit. There needed to be enough physical and mental capacity in him to actually achieve his goal.

I took Andrew out to a park to do an assessment. He needed to gain at least two seconds to be able to participate in the state championships in the category he'd set his mind on achieving. Two seconds isn't much, but in swimming it's a big deal.

"I want you to run as fast as you can for ten seconds," I instructed him. We marked off a certain distance, and he gave a full-out pursuit. I said, "Great. Now I want you to go back and run the same distance, two seconds faster." He looked at me like I was crazy. I repeated, "Now I want you to go run it two seconds faster. Go!"

He came back huffing and puffing after he'd run full speed. And guess what? He ran the distance in eight seconds. You would have thought this kid had just won a world championship! He was so thrilled that he had pushed himself to the limit and outdone himself. I could tell he had it within him to compete. He was able to push his body and reach a goal by pressing himself to the fullest extent. He simply needed the power of coaching to bring it out of him.

As we began to work through his champion zones, I realized he actually didn't believe he'd be able to maintain his endurance if he swam faster. Everything for Andrew in his physical fitness zone was a matter of endurance. The more I worked with him, the more I realized how his capacity to increase his endurance was key to qualifying for state championship.

Competing in the championship depended to a large extent upon his belief system as well. We came up with a Champion's Way process that completely focused on endurance: how he thought about it, what he believed about it, how he saw himself. I coached him to get a feel for what it was like to swim at a certain speed, and then what it felt like to go faster. He gained a lot of self-awareness in that area. He also took lessons for improving his stroke and increasing his speed and endurance.

At my request, he picked out a song. "Unstoppable" was his choice, his favorite song. It keyed into his whole mental-emotional state. He began to believe in himself. He was just as dedicated to developing his inner champion as he was to improving his physical endurance. Andrew was also a person of faith, so he started some spiritual meditations. That also propelled him forward.

Right in the middle of his training, I discovered he was going on vacation. "Coach Veronica," he said, "I'm not going to be able to do my training because I'm going on vacation."

I said, "Oh no, there is no championship without training. You are going to stay in training. You need to stay fully engaged in your process all the way to your competition. You've got to find a way to work in your training while you're on vacation."

During his getaway he found a swimming club and was also able to take some extra lessons and push himself even harder. In fact, it was during his vacation training that he had his biggest breakthroughs.

He shared a testimony of his progress: "Coach Veronica gave me confidence through a process, instead of through scores or times. We broke things down into champion zones. My favorite part was that it added a spiritual aspect to my training. I had never done this before. I actually believe it's one of the reasons why the other things didn't work. We identified a problem in each zone and then set a process to fix those problems. I had three weeks

50

until my next competition. To deal with my problem of fear, my dad gave me some special encouragement and wisdom about overcoming fear each day. That brought me closer to my dad as well. I found a renewed passion and motivation for my sport. I stepped up my physical training by running and going to the pool to train outside of practice. Then we also met one-on-one."

Andrew not only qualified for one race, but four! In each race he achieved a personal best. He explained, "I swam to all the best times in my races. I was so excited. Now that I saw how the process worked, I had 100 percent confidence."

His last testimony was beautiful. He said, "If someone had told me just a few months ago I was going to earn four cuts to go to JO's (Junior Olympics), I never would have believed them. It was amazing to see how the champion processes helped me achieve what I originally thought to be impossible." As we focused on his endurance from all angles, he accomplished what he had thought was impossible.

While I don't play competitive golf year-round anymore, I used to play the Futures Tour off and on for about five years. My career highlight was playing in the Women's U.S. Open.

I also love training for the seeming impossible. Because I still have a competitor in me, I try qualifying for the U.S. Open every year. Several years ago, it was held in Pinehurst. Since I was living in Pinehurst at the time, I thought, "I can't not try to qualify." The one-day qualifying tournament would be a grueling thirty-six holes. As I began to break down the physical components of that day, I saw that I would have to walk the equivalent of eight miles.

I wasn't even walking two miles at the time. I started my training months before the tournament so I would be able to walk up to eight miles in one day. A couple of weeks before the event, I carried my bag on the golf course so that I would have the endurance and physical strength to be able to perform. I worked on different parts of my golf swing as well as the processes of the other champion zones.

When the day came, I didn't qualify for the U.S. Open. However, because I followed *The Champion's Way* to my championship quest, I was able to evaluate my performance from a personal-growth perspective. Each zone is scored from 1 to 10. You chart where you start, and then you can see your progress. In my case, I scored a 3 in my physical zone when I began my training. After the qualifier, I scored myself an overall 8, since I was able to walk an impressive eight miles in one day. Instead of feeling like a failure, I could see how much progress I had made. If I had looked only at my score, I would have been judging myself from a narrow "success or fail" paradigm. By developing a continuum of progress instead, I could go back and assess my development in each zone. I achieved my new swing mechanics about thirty percent of the time.

When you adopt this process, you can largely eliminate failure because you're going along a growth continuum.

Consider how *The Champion's Way* relates to developing academic champions. I've coached thousands of students to succeed in academics. It's the same process. I often find that students who are labeled ADD and ADHD are mislabeled. They've never been taught how to become fully engaged in their studies. Students became empowered when they applied a system I created called "study cycles." A study cycle is a strategic, time-limited space where you apply each of the champion zones to do your work.

Andre was a bright but struggling student athlete from Jamaica attending Duke University. He came to me for help. Andre had just been labeled ADHD. I told him, "You know what you need? You need a study cycle."

In Jamaica, learning took place in a much more laid-back environment than at a high-end, competitive school like Duke. In Jamaica, there was a freedom to learn without a lot of pressure. When he arrived at Duke, he was met with intense pressure to perform, something he had never experienced before in his culture. As a result, he began to wig out.

"You're going to have to make a decision to free yourself and go back to the way your culture was in Jamaica," I said. "It's going to be anti-culture at Duke, but that's who you are. I'll help you set up some study cycles."

We set up a two-hour cycle for him. He would start with the physical:

1. Jog for twenty minutes before or after class.

2. Meditate for fifteen minutes.

3. Study for sixty minutes.

4. Socialize for twenty-five minutes.

Within a two-hour period, he worked through each of the champion zones. He became laser-focused on his study cycles, which he repeated two or three times a day.

Andre wrote me a note regarding his progress. He said, "Coach Veronica, I have had more concentration and more focus in one day using this study cycle system than I have had from all the resources I've tapped at my university for help."

Identifying his processes in each zone, starting with the physical, enabled him to fully engage in his studies with a new-found capacity to concentrate on his schoolwork. Andre was able to break through his ADHD label and achieve a peak performance in academics at Duke.

I want to encourage you. What physical process do you need to adopt with regard to your goal to help move you ahead? What swing mechanics do you need to develop? Mechanics can refer to your sport or the technical skills on your job.

I have found that you must have a certain amount of skill as a baseline for building on the other zones and processes. Without some skill mastery, you'll have difficulty being confident. Even saying, "I'm going to take one part of my sport and master this shot. I'm going to master this part of the game," is a good place to begin.

Be sure to pick out a clear process in the physical zone based on your personal level of development. Don't compare yourself to someone else who may be farther down the road than you. You can't start where you're not at. You can only start with where you are! It might be fitness, nutrition, swing mechanics, or whatever. Just pick one. Start where you are and move from there.

Finally, the more I coach, the more I realize there is a unique energetic bent to each athlete. Let me explain.

I coached a golfer wanting to become a high-level competitor. She was extremely power-driven. While she could hit the ball a long way, she had no finesse. She would get 100 yards and in from the green, and hit her wedge as if it were a driver. We had to work on pulling back her energy. I wanted her to become conscious of how much force she actually put into her shot.

Assessing and shifting your energy is also a part of the physical zone.

There may be a physical part of your sport that requires you to make your shots with finesse, with feel. Your energy comes from a completely different place in those instances.

To implement the physical zone, pick a process that you would like to develop. Then choose a practice to achieve the process.

Maybe you want to work on your endurance. In that case your goal might be, "I'll work on my endurance so I'll have enough stamina to play eighteen holes." To work on your endurance, you would establish a practice of walking a half-mile three days a week. After the first week, walk a mile three times the second week. That's an example of a practice behind a process.

You will be well on your Champion's Way to being physically energized as you fully engage in the physical zone of your training.

MODULE 5 WORKSHEET

This module is about the physical zone. The physical zone is made up of swing mechanics, nutrition, energy management, and fitness.

1. What elements of fitness do you most need to focus on?

   _____ Flexibility _____ Endurance _____ Speed

   _____ Power _____ Balance _____ Strength

2. What swing mechanic(s) are you working on? What do you need to improve to play your best game?

3. How does working on swing mechanics affect your play? Do you have a strategy for moving from mechanics to playing the game?

4. How well can you move from the practice tee to the playing tee?

5. Describe your experience and how well you do in both practice and play:

6. Describe a time when you were not thinking about swing mechanics at all and the effect it had on your game:

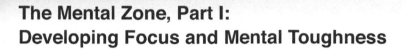

THE CHAMPION'S WAY

MODULE 6

The Mental Zone, Part I:
Developing Focus and Mental Toughness

The mental zone is one of my favorites. It's the place where you need to develop self-awareness about your thoughts. Most people are not conscious about what their thoughts are, those voices going around inside their heads.

The mental zone is all about focus, concentration, and champion mindsets. A mindset is a certain way of thinking about something. As we've said, champions think differently from other people. The more you can think like a champion, the more you will become one.

In this module, the focus and concentration piece comes to the forefront. Here's the mindset that I wish most for you: champions have mental toughness. Particularly at the beginning or midway through their journey, it's the one piece competitors seem to be lacking. Mental toughness is a necessary and vital key to winning and releasing your inner champion.

I'm going to give you a surefire way to create mental toughness. Of course, you'll have to hone it. I'll describe what mental toughness is, what it means to be in the zone, and how you can truly begin to take a leap in your peak performance by becoming mentally tough. This will also improve your focus and concentration.

Here's what you must understand: peak performance happens only from a totally positive place in your head. One negative thought can destroy a peak performance. Think of taking some red food coloring and putting one drop in a clear glass of water. That one drop affects the whole glassful.

You might be hitting a shot across the water to the green. Just one thought of fear affects your whole focus and concentration. That one negative thought can destroy a peak performance. Then, if you don't know how to quickly let go of a bad shot, it can easily spiral. You'll take that energy into your next shots, regardless of what sport you're in. You need to be able to create a way to speedily release a bad shot. Two things need to happen first: you must understand how peak performance happens and how mental toughness is created in order to perform at your best.

I want to repeat this: peak performance happens from a totally positive place in your head. One negative thought can destroy your peak performance. How can you intentionally create a place in your head that's totally positive?

In performance coaching, this state of being in which there is flow is called an ideal performance state, or I-P-S. I learned about this concept from Dr. James Loehr, a world-renowned peak performance expert. Think of a square. Everything inside that square is your ideal performance state, and it is totally positive. (See the worksheet at the end of this module.)

In your ideal performance state, begin to define words, terms, and emotions to write inside the box. When you're doing your best, when you're in that place where flow and peak performance is happening, how would you describe the mental-emotional place in your head? It is positive. It is exciting. It is calm, a place of concentration. In fact, the most accurate term to describe an ideal performance state is calm concentration. (We'll talk about the emotional side of this term in the next module.)

The problem is, we have all kinds of voices going on in our head that attempt to destroy our ideal performance state. I believe your natural state is positive. We want to begin to create some protection around your ideal performance state so that all negative thoughts are considered to be intruders. Think about it. If your natural state is positive, it's easier to think about keeping out negativity than it is to think about producing a completely positive state. Here's another way to consider it—when you leave your positive state of mind, just return to it. Consider "calm concentration" to be your mental-emotional "home." You want to learn how to guard your home!

If somebody came to your front door and said, "Let me in, because I want to steal all your money," what would you do? You would slam the door shut.

The whole idea around mental toughness is to create a stronger internal voice than an external voice. In order to do that, you have to create a strong internal fence to keep out all the negative thoughts that would invade your positive mental-emotional mindset.

Let's go back to my first major championship. I was playing the seventh-ranked amateur of the United States. When it came down to where the rubber met the road, where I had to make a decision in the heat of battle, whose voice did I listen to? Did I stand in my own space and claim my own voice? No, I listened to my opponent's voice.

I want you to become aware that you actually have three voices going on inside your head pretty much all the time. We need to be able to identify those three voices. Then we can begin to speak out of the strongest one, pushing back and closing the door to the negative one. We actually will begin to create an ideal performance state when we do that, separating the voices out of what I call "the battle within." In sports, as well as in life, you have to keep the battle on the outside. The moment you internalize the battle, you've lost.

We are going to create an ideal performance state that will result in an abundance of mental toughness. First, however, let me identify those three voices.

The first is called "the critic." We all have that voice that says, "You can't. You won't. Who do you think you are?" That's the negative, critical voice that shuts down your mind. Bottom line, it's the voice that says "No!"

In the introductory module, I talked about how passion and focus are the two distinguishing features of champions. For you to reach peak performance, you must take the clamps off your negative thinking. That way, you can discover new possibilities for yourself. Begin to identify what those critical voices are going on inside your head. What exact thought do you have out there in the middle of competition that's putting the clamps on your brain? That is your critical voice. Write it down just like you say it to yourself.

There's a second voice, too. It's called the coaching voice. That's the voice that says, "Why not? What if you could hit the shot? I can do this. I believe in myself. I've done this before." It is a supportive, empowering voice. Sometimes it's a question that opens up your mind to a new possibility, like "What would happen if I did believe in my dream? What would be the first step toward it?"

By the way, this is a very important voice for parents to detect in themselves. You might not realize it, but when you're using your critical voice, you're actually shutting down your player's performance instead of building them up. Here's a common truth in peak performance coaching: for every negative, critical thing you say to somebody, you need to say five positive things to keep up your player's confidence level.

There was once a study with the top basketball coaches in the country. The question was asked, "What is it that creates champions?" The result was interesting. Apparently it was not all that important for someone to be out there helping players to win. It was discovered that just getting the players out on the court with confidence put them in a position to win.

Parents and coaches, when you are dealing with your players, keep that in mind. You don't want to shut down their minds. You want to open up their minds to new possibilities. You do that by using an empowering, supportive, you-can-do-this voice, which also includes asking powerful questions.

Besides the critical voice and coaching voice, there's a third: I call this the champion voice. It's the voice that says, "I will play from a place of victory. I don't care what I shoot. When I step up on that first tee, when I enter the game, when the clock goes off to play, I'm playing from a place of victory. I will not be defeated. Defeat is not a part of who I am." Bottom line, it's the voice that says, "I can and I will." It's the voice that not only affirms your highest self, but steps out and takes action to move forward. It's your "Go!" voice. It's your "Let's do this!" voice. It's the voice that is fully committed to your dream and launches you into immediate action, however big or small that step may be.

I watched *Dancing with the Stars* the same season Ryan Lochte, the Olympian swimmer, was a contestant. Prior to that, he'd been involved in a situation that revealed his character in a not-so-great light. As a result, he was given a lot of scrutiny, with many public voices speaking against him.

He was interviewed after one of the *Dancing with the Stars* episodes. They were discussing the courage it took for him to go on the television show after his mishap following the Olympics. His immediate response was, "I'm an Olympian. I don't quit!" His emphatic words came flying out of his mouth.

There was a champion voice in Ryan's response. Did you hear it? "Champions don't quit." It was in his bones. That is the voice of the champion. You have the critic voice. You have the coach voice, and you have the champion voice. Which one do you listen to the most? You will never release your inner champion listening to your critical voice that puts you down. You'll only release your inner champion by affirming your best self—by speaking from your champion identity. Despite Ryan's mistake, he still spoke from his champion voice when challenged.

Here's an example to show you how to move from one voice to the other. To have mental toughness, you must not only be able to identify the voice, you also have to be able to change the voice from critic to champion as quickly as possible.

One year I was trying to decide whether to pursue a certain championship. Since I was working, I would have to take time out to pursue it. I wanted to be sure it was an authentic dream. For me it came down to deciding if I wanted to dedicate myself to the training required to try to qualify for the U.S. Open.

Here's what my critical voice sounded like: "You can't do that. You have swing faults. You don't have the swing to do that."

A certain element of that was true. I did indeed have a swing fault that needed to be fixed. A great deal of judgment was wrapped around that as well. The critical voice inside closed down my mind. It closed off even the possibility of my trying to qualify and play in the championship.

As I began to recognize the critical voice, I switched to my coaching voice, which asked powerful questions. It made observations without judgment. The coaching voice said, "What is the first obstacle you would need to overcome in the pursuit of your championship? How would you even realize if it's an authentic dream?" Suddenly the clamps came off my mind, and my thinking opened up. I answered, "I'd have to fix this part of my swing so I could perform under pressure."

The next question followed: "Who would you go to?" Immediately the answer came. "I would go to Warren, who helped me earlier this year. He seemed to really be able to help me with that certain swing fault."

Again, the critic spoke: "But he's in another state. Right now he charges outside your budget." The coach replied, "Why don't you just write to him? Be vulnerable and transparent. Tell him your dream. Just see if he might be willing to help you."

At last the champion voice stepped up. "Would I do it, or wouldn't I? Would I rise to the occasion? Would I explore the possibility, or wouldn't I?" My champion voice decided to speak, "Yes! I am going to DO IT!"

So, I sat down one night and wrote to Warren. "I know that you are in another state far from me. I know that I probably can't afford you right now, but here's my dream. I want to qualify for the Women's U.S. Open. You really helped me in the past. I'm wondering if you would consider helping me again." I emailed him in faith.

He wrote me back, saying, "If you can come next weekend, I'm going to be in a state next door to yours. Drive over, and I will help you for the afternoon for free."

My inner champion was instantly activated. There was something I wanted to know. I asked him, "Is this an authentic pursuit? Would you validate the possibility that I could do this?" He said, "Absolutely."

That year I pursued it. I didn't qualify, but it didn't matter: I was on the road to championship. I was so proud that I had listened to my champion voice.

Begin to discern the differences between your critical voice, your coaching voice, and your inner champion voice.

Particularly when you're out performing, begin to identify your critical, judgmental voice. This is the intruder. You must consider all negative thoughts spoken by your critical voice to be intruders. Do not accept them.

You can shut these intruders out by creating what is called a mental trigger. A mental trigger is an internal fence that you build around your mind to separate the negative thoughts from the positive thoughts. It's simply a signal like a doorbell. It says, "Somebody is knocking at your door," and you want to be sure that door is shut. There are different ways to create mental triggers for ensuring your internal voice is greater than your external one.

Let me give you a few examples. First is an athlete who created her own ideal performance state. I asked her to write down all her negative, critical thoughts exactly as she experienced them. Then I had her write down all of her empowering thoughts, the coach, and the champion thoughts that came in. That way she could begin to separate and identify the different voices.

Critical voices coming against her in her competitions included:

You can do way better than this. Oh, come on. When will it work out for me? I don't trust it. I can't reach my goal. I can't. Why I can't I do this? I never win. Will I ever hit this shot? Will I ever hit it right? Why did I do that? I'm unlucky. That's going to hurt.

I even had one golfer say: I should have taken up volleyball. I knew it.

There is so much negativity here!

In her ideal performance state, this is what she wrote:

The plan worked. I won. I did it. Confidence. Enjoyment. Excitement. Belief.

When you can recognize the difference between the voices, you are in a much better position to make a choice. When the critical voice comes up in competition—usually accompanied by fear—you can gain confidence in shutting it down.

Instead of sitting down and having lunch with the negative thought, I recommend not entertaining the conversation at all. Just use your mental trigger.

Here's an example of a mental trigger. Recall Lexi's story. In her case, when her bad shot came and she hit it, instead of spiraling out, she flicked it off. It was a trigger for her to say, "I'm letting it go. I am not going to internalize that negativity. Bye-bye!"

I had a student, a lady pro who was trying to qualify for the U.S. Open. We examined what happened when she became fearful. She had the skillset to qualify, but fear was holding her back.

When she was growing up, she liked to play with toy guns. Since it was already part of her experience, we came up with a mental trigger that whenever a negative thought came to her, she would take her right hand, point it to the ground like she was shooting a gun, and say "Pow! Pow! I'm shooting you down!"

It was hysterical. When she did that on the course, she would burst out in a smile. Her mental trigger shifted her fearful emotional state to positivity— immediately. She was then able to easily return to her ideal performance state. She successfully made it through the first qualifier.

You can use a "finger gun" to shoot down your critical thought, or you can "flick it off" as you would a mosquito for your mental trigger. I had one student make up her own mental trigger. She called it, "Whoosh go!" Instead of spiraling down and keeping the bad shot in her head, she would say, "Whoosh!" It would go right through her—"Whoosh, go." It's that simple and powerful. A mental trigger is a short verbal cue and action which together create a forceful boundary line to your thoughts. It empowers you to take charge of your thoughts instead of your thoughts taking charge of you.

In many of my workshops, I show the participants what I call "the fifteenth club." It's a sword. The whole idea of this is to evoke your imagination and produce a picture. Something that's visceral is a lot stronger than just having a mental thought.

I lift up the sword and with a strong force, make a forceful, thrashing move. You know what a sword does, right? It cuts away all the negative energy and clears the negative atmosphere around you. I give a plastic sword to each student and have them use it on the tee before they swing the club to clear away all negativity. It's a strong and fun practice to establish an ideal performance state before you hit your shot.

When you're working on mental toughness, find an object similar to a sword, or get a plastic sword from the dollar store or Walmart. Make it your fifteenth club. Invoke your imagination. When those undesirable thoughts come up, slash them away immediately. Not only will you be forming the practice of mental toughness, you'll have fun doing it, too!

I had one student say, "Yeah, when all that negativity came up on the golf course, I just considered that voice to be my evil twin sister. I said, 'Shut up and go home today. I'm not talking to you today.'" The whole idea is to create a forceful mental trigger that lets negativity you are not entertaining that voice today. It will help you to separate the negative thought from who you are. Remember, it's an intruder.

Let me put it this way: thoughts produce emotions. Anything you perceive as a threat is going to evoke a negative emotion. Anything you perceive as a challenge is going to evoke a positive emotion. You must have mastery over your thoughts. Again, one of the best ways to do that is to go back and think about your thoughts. Maybe you have to do it after your round. Think about what thought produced that shot, not just about how you made your swing.

Many people say, "I just have trouble hitting the green," or "I just didn't make the stroke." No, something in your head contributed to that. If you were fearful, just ask yourself, "What were you thinking? Were you functioning from an ideal performance state of calm concentration? Did you use a mental trigger? Were you aware of that? Did you implement it?"

Come up with your own mental trigger. Then implement it. This can be done even with your schoolwork. It can be done in a relationship. You're creating a boundary by stating, "I am going to remain in a place of positivity and calmness, because that's my ideal performance state."

Remember, *The Champion's Way* includes creating mental toughness by discerning what voices are going on, then moving from the critic to the coach to the champion. It all begins with making observations without judgment. It removes the thinker from the thoughts. It allows you to stand back and just observe your thoughts. That way, you can move to a place of a positive thought versus a negative one.

I once had a young student, Lotte. She was an aspiring junior golfer. However, after a bad shot she started to get emotional. She became angry.

In working through all of the zones, we discovered that her over-focus on score—just thinking about her score--actually caused her to shoot higher scores.

We set about to make a distinction. What was she was going to think about on the course? What wasn't she going to think about while on the course? This is so simple, but it's also very powerful. If you can begin to determine what your ideal performance state is versus your non-ideal state, you can begin to create appropriate boundaries. If you can define something, you can go there. If you can't, your mind has nowhere to go. Your mind has to be directed to a target—especially in your thoughts.

She said, "I always have something to think about on the course. Some thoughts are necessary, some are unnecessary. From these experiences I can figure out what to think about, what not to think about."

Here's what she defined for herself:

Think: Present. Let go of all past shots, good or bad. Focus just on the present shot that's about to be hit. It should be the only shot that is important to you. For me, it's a song. This helps keep my mind off my score. Again the current shot.

Not think: Past shots. Future score that you would like. Let the score happen. Don't focus on it. If you force it, focus will be lost, and the score you wanted will not occur. Your opponent's score—let her worry about that. On your current score, let it flow through your mind. If you think about it, you'll begin to think about impossible targets: three birdies to get rid of a triple, which will frustrate you when you score higher.

She came up with her own powerful mental game plan to stay in her ideal performance state. It helped her not to think about score so she could be emotionally present for her shot. It included singing a song. She intentionally told her mind how to think. It worked because you can't think of two thoughts at the same time. It's impossible.

If you're singing a song, you can't be negative. It also included talking to her playing partners once she walked off the tee. If you're in conversation, you're not going to allow your critical voice to come forward.

If you're intentionally thinking about what you want to think about, you will not be thinking about what you don't want to think about.

Because she had obtained this heightened state of mental clarity, I knew she was going to go out and win her next tournament.

Here's her happy surprise. She not only won the next tournament, she won every match in every tournament for two months straight. She was an amazing example of calm concentration. It started with the mental awareness of her own thoughts, claiming her own voice, standing in that and walking it out—all the way to victory.

I encourage you to become clear about what your thoughts are. Create your mental trigger and you too will have much greater clarity, focus, and mental toughness.

Find a big piece of paper and draw a big square in the middle. On top of the box, write "I.P.S." In the box, list all the thoughts and emotions that come to you when you're in your ideal performance state. Next, list all those negative thoughts, just as they are, outside of the box and all around it. Identify them and write them just as you say them to yourself. Then come up with a mental trigger that keeps the good thoughts in and the bad thoughts out. Write on the lines of the box itself what your mental trigger is and how you're going to use it. That's your mental fence line. (You can use the worksheet at the end of this module.)

Now you're on the road to championship with *The Champion's Way* to focus, concentration, mental toughness, and victory!

MODULE 6 WORKSHEET

1. Peak performance happens from a totally _____ place in your head. Just one _____ thought can destroy a peak performance.

2. Mental toughness is created when you can intentionally create an inner state emotionally and mentally that is totally _____.

3. This inner state is called your Ideal Performance _____.

4. The three voices that speak to you are the _____ voice, the _____ voice, and the _____ voice. Which one do you want to speak the loudest? Circle it.

5. Let's create your Ideal Performance State. On the next page is a square. (*See Figure 6.1 on page 70.*) Inside the square is your ideal performance state. The square is an internal mental fence you create to separate the positive thought from the negative thoughts which are located outside the box.

   A. Write in the box all the POSITIVE words that describe your ideal performance state. For me, I would write joy, confidence, excitement, calm concentration, belief, knowing. Write the words that describe your personal state when you are in the flow.

   B. Write the EXACT thoughts that come to your mind—exactly what you say to yourself when the negative thoughts come to mind. Examples might be: "Why did I ever take up this game? I should quit." Another may be, "I'll never win." Yet another may be, "I hate myself." Write this outside of your I.P.S. box.

C. Now create a mental trigger, something you will do or say that will keep the negative thought from coming into your I.P.S. box. It may be to flick off the negative thought or to shoot it down. It may be something you say. Just pick one and begin to implement it on the course. Mental toughness is created when your internal voice is stronger than your external voice. The idea is to treat the negative thought as an intruder and keep it at bay at all costs!! Write down your mental trigger right on the line of the box.

This exercise is designed for you to gain self-awareness of your thoughts, both positive and negative. It's to help you begin to assert your authority over your negative voice and to hold to your positive voice.

Figure 6.1

Negative Thought:

Negative Thought:

Mental Trigger:

Ideal Performance State:

Write down your positive words that describe FLOW

Negative Thought:

Negative Thought:

THE CHAMPION'S WAY

MODULE 7

The Mental Zone, Part II: Champion Mindsets

The second mental zone module is all about champion mindsets. As I've said throughout this training, champion thinking is different from ordinary thinking. The way you think very much determines how you go about your competitive journey, how you prepare for and perform in your competition, and also how you bring yourself up to the highest level.

I love being around champions: they call me up. I want to be in their atmosphere. I'm always amazed at how many people don't really care about making the changes required to call themselves up higher.

Whether you're on the front end, the middle end, or the back end of your competitive journey, don't ever be afraid to give yourself permission to make changes in your thinking, your habits, and your mindset. Advancing down the championship road begins with your mindset.

What is a mindset? Quite simply, it is how you have set your mind to think about something. For instance, if you truly believe you can't do something, you actually have mental clamps on your brain, and you will end up not doing it.

I was giving a lesson to a lady one day, trying to help her release her hands through the shot. She wouldn't believe that the hands worked in the way I was showing her. No amount of hands-on-help would change how she did things, until I stopped and said, "Listen. Would you just open up your mind for the sake of learning what I'm telling you?" I had to open up her mind to remove the mindset that was shutting her down.

Once she finally opened her mind, she hit the most amazing shot. She jumped up and down and twirled around. All of a sudden, she was receptive to learning something new. It didn't happen, however, until I addressed her limiting beliefs and cemented mindset.

The beautiful part about teaching young folks is that they are impressionable. They can immediately adopt a new mindset. Once people get older and stuck in habitual thinking, they have to reset their mind. It's harder to undo a mindset that's already set in a different direction.

I'm going to list some champion mindsets for you. Once you know how champions think and what their mindsets are, you can select one champion mindset a week, meditate on it, and apply it for yourself to level up your thinking.

Here's the first champion mindset on my list: **Champions master processes.** I have a friend, Dr. Richard Coop. He was one of the founding members of the sport psychology movement. He shared that one time he was at a dinner listening to a conversation between Jack Nicklaus and Coach Dean Smith, the Hall of Fame coach for the University of North Carolina basketball team. Both of these men are amazing champions; in fact, each is a champion of champions. They were talking about peak performance and championships. Dr. Coop said, "They never once talked about winning. All they talked about was mastering processes."

Coach Smith spoke about his practice of hiring coaches to come in during practice games to act as referees, just as if they were in a real game playing under pressure. They would practice in such a way that that practice imitated what they would actually do in a real game. Jack talked about the different shots he had mastered, like the one-iron shot, and about his ability to hit a fade or a draw. Both of these champion men focused on practices that would help them to master processes.

Whether you're a beginner or whether you're advanced, pick a process to master. If you're a beginner, the process would be learning to master aligning to a shot. If you're an executive, it might be mastering the process of selling or the process of giving yourself permission to develop a new skill or pursue a dream, even if you think of yourself as older. Maybe it means giving yourself permission to master a shot. You're a champion when you master a process.

Champions more quickly release a bad shot than other competitors.
They can get back into that zone, their ideal performance state, more quickly
than others.

In the next competition, take some time to say, "I am going to be someone
who can quickly release a bad shot." That works with relationships too.
How quick are you to forgive? How quick are you to release that person
from judgment? If you can stay in a judgment-free zone, particularly against
yourself and others, you are being a champion.

Champions have emotional mastery. This is so important for you to work
on. You've got to be able to master your emotions.

Perhaps you have a problem with anger. Make a decision that you're going
to conquer that unhealthy emotional imbalance. You're going to figure it out
and apply a process of overcoming it. Give yourself a score from one to ten.
Your beginning score, maybe it's a three, and you're going to move it to a ten.
How will you do that? You need to be able to focus on it, because what you
focus on expands.

When you intentionally work on mastering your emotions, you're being
a champion!

Champions have a system for debriefing their performances. We're
going to talk about this in the next module. You have to be able to learn from
your competitions. If you don't take time to debrief your performance, you'll
never deduce the real learning points from those experiences.

I still think Lance Armstrong was a great competitor, even though he had
a drug use problem and character issues. I remember reading some of his
books, where he was talking about the ability to separate his worth from his
performance. That way, he could look at his performance objectively to see
what he needed to tweak and improve. It's essential that you have a process
for debriefing your competitions. *The Champion's Way* will empower you to
capture the real win and let go of the rest.

**Champions have fewer thoughts than others and can sustain them
longer.** You have a vision to achieve a certain goal, but you're not there yet.

What distinguishes a champion from other people? The difference is the ability to envision an outcome, to put yourself energetically from the very start into the outcome you haven't even realized yet. That is the process of holding to a thought long enough, however long it takes, until that thought is realized. Sustaining a thought until it becomes a reality is a remarkable trait of a champion.

A champion vision of a goal could be something simple. It could be your saying, "I have a vision of seeing myself fit and healthy. I'm going to start off by walking three times a week as an initial goal." You keep envisioning yourself as fit and healthy, holding to that thought and applying the practice behind it until it is realized. Holding to a thought long enough until it's realized is a hard thing to do, but it's what distinguishes a champion from other achievers.

I remember when I went to graduate school. I wanted to see how well I could do and set a goal of achieving a 4.0 for a master's program I enrolled in. I had to hold to the thought, and then I had to carve out a system to do my work. I had to make a commitment to the process. I had to have a mindset, an ideal performance state, where I would allow nothing to interfere with my accomplishing the desired goal.

When I achieved my goal, I decided to do a second master's. I thought, "Oh, my gosh. Can I get another 4.0?" It seemed impossible, but I added my faith into the process. Again, to be able to hold to a thought for three years of training and be consistent with the process of going about achieving my goal was a remarkable thing. I did achieve my goal. However, I also realized that goal achievement does not necessarily bring you fulfillment. It might bring you a trophy and the most outstanding student award, but it might not bring you lasting joy.

If you would be a champion, it's crucial that. as you go about your work, you're able to hold to a thought. At the same time, realize that your goal may not necessarily bring you the fulfillment you desire. This is why another champion mindset is, "Champions inspire others." You want to use your platform to inspire others to come up higher. Adding value to others is what truly gives you meaning and fulfillment in what you do.

Many of my students who've gone through *The Champion's Way* process find other players suddenly saying, "Wow, did you notice that so-and-so had such amazing emotional calm? Look at her. Look at what she's achieved." The way they go about playing inspires other players to come up higher. Then they're able to introduce them to *The Champion's Way* of becoming a true champion. It's been a heartwarming thing for me to see.

Champions love to practice. Champions willingly and joyfully submit to training. A research study found that the happiest students on campus were athletes and musicians, and it was because they willingly submitted to training. Do you love to practice? Do you love the process of skill development and being teachable so you can submit to instruction? My most successful students have been the best learners. They were able to receive what I wanted to impart to them. Enjoy your process of training. That's how your potential is released.

Champions have coaches who fully release their potential. You cannot release your full potential without a coach. Every great achiever has coaches. Don't be afraid to invest in a coach. Be open and willing to submit to a coach who's there to help you.

Champions have superior focus. When you practice, do you take dead aim on a target? Is your focus so dialed in that your eye is on sinking the ball in the hole, not just getting it somewhere near the hole? How good are you at picking a specific target and channeling all your energy to that target? Are you able to clear your mind so that hundreds of people could be watching you, but you don't even know they are there? Can you prioritize your work, your studies, and your practice so that when you're engaged in one activity, your mind is focused only on that one activity? If you can exhibit superior focus, you are a champion!

If you're a student athlete, be careful to moderate things that will sabotage your ability to focus. You need to be able to focus on your goals, achieve them, and fully concentrate on a certain subject. Studies have shown that too much time playing computer games actually affects your ability to focus. If you want to be a champion, ration out how much time you spend with your head in the computer. Even too much time on social media can distract you and steal away your practice of "superior focus."

Champions have superior passion. You have got to have a "want-to" mindset. When you're passionate about your sport, your love for the game will propel you to spend the time it takes to train and become the best you can be. When you join focus with passion, you have a winning combination.

Champions function from a determined state. You have to be determined to go after a goal. I once had a student who wanted a scholarship to go to college, yet her work ethic suffered. She had to be told to work. When she began to see that if she worked harder, improved her game and her scores, she would have a better chance. I encouraged her to take the initiative to call some college coaches herself. In the end, she got a fine scholarship to a college, and it changed her. She realized that through hard work, she could achieve her goals. What made the difference was her functioning from a determined, not passive, state.

Champions measure their performance and progress. There is no progress without measurement. You must keep a record of your stats. You have to look at them and say, "I suffer here, I can do better there." Whether the goal you are pursuing is academic, athletic, or something else, having those statistics will help you greatly. They will form a roadmap for you as you track your measurements.

Champions can turn a disempowering emotion into an empowering emotion at will. Think about that. The people that lose it emotionally and stay there will never become champions. So much depends on how you use recovery time, positively or negatively, between shots. That will affect your performance. You want to be able to quickly transform a disempowering emotion into an empowering one at will. We'll talk about that in the next module.

Champions perform from a place of rest. If you recall, I mentioned in Module 5 how Tiger Wood's father, Earl, would tell his son after a championship that if he needed to sleep for twelve hours, he should do so. He knew his body needed restoration. He also knew that peak performance happens from a place of rest. You need to be sure to get adequate sleep so you're in a place of strength.

Champions are bent on conquest. This resonates with me. If you have a champion spirit, you love to go all out in pursuit of a thing. You are after that trophy. Even if you're not a winner yet, you are pressing toward that mark. You love the hunt.

I love this one too: **True champions speak to the champion in others.** I encourage all of my students to be role models of encouragement and to inspire other players. We need one another. We need to call each other up and say, "Hey, you're really great at that." We all need the validation of someone speaking to our potential.

Parents often criticize their children in sports and other areas of life. If they would just speak to the champion in the child, "I know you can do this. If you work hard, there's no doubt in my mind that you can accomplish that," you would be calling out the champion in them. Young people tend not to have adult disciplines formed in them yet. At times, I see parents criticizing their kids when those internal qualities haven't been developed. Nothing has been formed in them yet that they can respond to. You must take a thoughtful coaching approach so as to elevate and empower them in these mindsets. They have to be formed.

Champions see themselves as champions. Even if you don't feel you can win yet, do you walk tall? Do you talk tall? How do you carry yourself? You can always spot a champion in the way they think, the way they move, and the way they treat one another. Let me share a couple of examples of champion formation resulting from my efforts to help equip these players to think like champions.

A mom called me. Her son was going to be playing in a big championship. She said, "He's unmotivated and unfocused, but do you think you could help me?"

I replied, "Sure." I had never seen him swing. I had never met him in person, but we had two Skype sessions.

I knew if he was going to perform well, he must get superior-focused. I would have to open up his mind to a new possibility in his life.

We did one Skype session on passion. I had him write down every single reason why he thought he could win. That is what champions do—they think about winning. Then I did a session on focus. I got very specific about setting goals in his practice time. I gave him a two-hour, highly specific practice session to do.

Before long, he had opened his mind to a new possibility. He took aim on a target. In two weeks' time, this twelve-year-old went out and shot a 66, winning him a big Canadian junior tournament. All he did was adopt champion mindsets and some champion practices, which took him to a whole new level of play.

I mentioned Lotte in the last module. When I saw that she'd gotten herself to a place where she could win and she started winning, we began to strategize her high school season. Looking at the whole picture, I said, "You are in a position to win every single match."

 Now whether she could or not, we didn't know. However, we wanted to open up her mind to a new possibility of taking her championship to a higher level. One of the ways we began to work on that was through an image. We created a simple picture. To me, this is just a stunning image that aided her in meditating on the thought of winning every match.
The line of little trophies elevated her thinking and opened up her mind to a whole new level. The good news is, she won half of her matches. Though she didn't win them all, she was able to focus on winning. She directed her mind in a brand new way that she'd never considered before.

Champions do think about winning. For many people, that's not even in their mind. The mindset of winning has to be cultivated.

This is what Lotte said when she began to win: "Winning not only changes me as a golfer but also how I think of the game. After my win, I feel like a champion who can achieve her goals one step at a time. I now feel I can achieve anything, whether it means reaching harder goals, playing against strong competitors, or making friends at a new high school." Notice that she even took her champion mindsets into a place that could be intimidating—going to a new school. In place of that, she empowered herself to know that she could accomplish going to the new school without being intimidated.

"Winning makes me think about playing the game without focusing on score. I think about what I have done well in, and currently it changes the way I think about the sport," she said. Lotte has a champion mindset.

Here is another one of her quips: "I am a champion because there is no quit in me. When others were withdrawing because of high heat and scores, quitting is unthinkable to me. Having a no-quit attitude makes me a true champion." She was defining herself as a champion with her champion mindsets based on who she is.

Another time I helped a champion student named David Dean. He reached out to me on the internet. He was an undergraduate and had a dream of going to medical school to become a neurosurgeon. While he was a good student, he was not a great student. However, he had a very strong sense of who he was.

He told me he was weak in writing, so I equipped him with the mechanics of being a competent writer. That was the mechanics part, the physical part of being a student.

He applied what I taught him. When he came back, he said, "I just took a test. Sixty percent of the class dropped the class because they had a failing grade." The average grade was 59, but he made a 91. He said, "Coach Veronica, do you think I could go to the head of the class?"

"Why not? If you have that thought, it is possible, and I will help you," I told him.

 I continued to equip David with the mechanics of good academic writing and to encourage him. On his next test, he made 100 in his pharmacology class. Within one semester's time, David advanced to the head of the class. Then, he not only received a distinguished student award from the faculty, but he was co-published as an undergrad, something absolutely unheard of. He began to tell other students about the peace and joy he had, and how to achieve it. He began to inspire them. Upon graduation, he was awarded a full PhD scholarship in neuroscience.

His is an amazing story. This twenty-one-year-old started from a place of being better than average, but struggling. When he began to equip himself with champion mindsets and fully applied himself, he busted loose to realize his potential. He began to see himself as a champion and then performed like one. His faith in God also propelled him to achieve what he had thought was impossible. David Dean is a true champion.

I want to encourage you to open up your mind to a new possibility, to envision an outcome, to see yourself there, and to adopt champion mindsets. Your thinking determines everything. Pick a champion mindset. I don't care which one it is. Just pick one, focus on it, begin to practice it, and see your performance soar.

I believe in you.

MODULE 7 WORKSHEET

Champions think differently than others. In your champion development, give yourself _____ to make changes in your thinking, habits, and mindsets so you can advance down the road to championship.

What is a mindset? It is how you _____ your mind to think about something.

What is one mindset shift you have made since being in this course?

Champion Mindsets:

1. Champions _____ processes.

   Choose a process you're going to master. Write down the practice you will implement to begin to master it.

2. Champions more quickly _____ a bad shot than other players.

   How long does it take you to release a bad shot?

3. Champions have emotional _____.

4. Champions have a system for _____ performances.

5. Champions have fewer thoughts and can _____ them longer.

6. Champions have the ability to _____ an outcome.

   They can _____ to a thought long enough until that thought is realized.

What is the thought you are holding to?

What is the practice behind it that will help you to realize your thought?

It is important that your goals not only bring you a sense of achievement, but also a sense of _____.

7. Champions inspire _____.

8. Champions love to _____.

9. Champions have _____ who release their full potential. You cannot release your full potential without a

_____.

10. Champions have superior _____.

Don't spend too much time on your _____ because it will affect your ability to focus.

11. Champions have superior passion. You have to have a

_____.

12. Champions function from a determined state. You have to be

_____ to go after a goal.

13. Champions _____ their performance and progress.

14. Champions can turn a _____ emotion into an empowering emotion at will.

15. Champions perform from a place of _____.

16. Champions are _____ on conquest.

17. True champions speak to the _____ in others.

18. Champions see themselves as _____.

19. Champions think about winning. What does "winning" look like for you?

Circle the champion mindset that spoke to you the loudest. Choose to practice it. Write down the champion mindset you've chosen and how you're going to implement it. Set an intention to fully focus on it for the next two weeks specifically. Measure your progress.

COACHING ASSIGNMENT

Champions have superior focus and passion. To develop your potential as a champion, you have to come up a notch or two higher in your ability to focus and open up your mind to a new possibility, which releases passion. Here is an exercise to amplify your thinking to engage more fully in focus and passion:

PASSION: Review your declarations from MODULE 4 and write down the top five reasons why you believe you deserve to be in the champions' circle:

1._____

2._____

3._____

4._____

5._____

How are you coming along with meditating on your 3-by-5 card? Maybe it's been a few weeks, and you're ready to add another declaration to this card. Again, put it in three places where you interact with each day—like your mirror, desk, refrigerator, etc. Meditate on your truth for a few minutes, and make it a practice to reflect on your champion mindset.

FOCUS: It is not enough to open up your mind to a new possibility. You also have to take dead aim on a target and create more focus for yourself. This happens as you set specific goals within your practice. In golf, instead of hitting chip shots for fifteen minutes, set a goal to sink at least one chip shot within that fifteen-minute practice. Instead of just hitting on the driving range, form a fairway with boundaries on the range and hit ten drives within that fairway. Envision new outcomes, and then set goals and practices that will help you to achieve that outcome.

If your target is other than sports, such as personal life or business goals, write down some goals and practices that will take you to another level of focus.

Do both your PASSION and FOCUS exercises together, and you will release the champion within!

What one champion mindset will you adopt as your life-mindset this season?

What champion mindset will you put into practice this week?

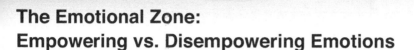

THE CHAMPION'S WAY

MODULE 8

The Emotional Zone:
Empowering vs. Disempowering Emotions

Emotions are the topic of this module. Up to this point, we've talked about the physical, the spiritual, and the mental. In many ways, the whole emotional realm that relates to performance is one of the most felt but least defined.

It's easy to define the physical zone. It's not quite so easy to define the emotional zone. One of the best ways to understand emotions and how they affect your performance is through a helpful grid. I refer to this grid as outlined by world-class performance expert Dr. James Loehr in his book *The Power of Full Engagement.* I highly recommend that you get this book.

Dr. Loehr provides a definition and an explanation of empowering versus disempowering emotions in a manner that specifically relates to your performance. Just as in the mental zone, where you distinguish positive versus negative thinking, in the emotional zone you distinguish between empowering versus disempowering emotions.

Take a look at Dr. Loehr's grid. Your emotions are divided up into four different categories.

Dynamics of Energy - Empowering vs. Disempowering Emotions:

High Negative	High Positive	
Angry	Invigorated	
Fearful	Confident	**Fully Engaged**
Anxious	Challenged	**Ideal Performance**
State Emotions	Joyful	
Defensive	Connected	
Resentful		

Low Negative	Low Positive
Depressed	Relaxed
Exhausted	Mellow
Burned Out	Peaceful
Hopeless	Tranquil
Defeated	Serene

We all have empowering and disempowering emotions. On the disempowering side, we have high-negative emotions: anger, fear, anxiety, defensiveness, and resentment. These are powerful, negative emotions that take power away from you as it relates to your performance.

When you're in the low-negative emotional quadrant, you feel depressed, exhausted, burned out, hopeless, and defeated. These are negative emotions that also steal from you, but they consist of more low-grade energy.

On the positive side, you have high-positive as well as low-positive emotions. High-positive is described as being invigorated, confident, challenged, joyful, and connected. On the low-positive side, your emotions are described as relaxed, mellow, peaceful, tranquil, and serene.

In which quadrant of this grid do you think peak performance happens? Does it happen when you're angry and fearful? No. Does it happen when you're depressed and exhausted? No. Does peak performance happen when you're relaxed and mellow? No. Peak performance happens in the high-positive zone marked by being invigorated, challenged, positive, excited, and joyful.

Take note of this. **You want to get into and remain in a high-positive zone to experience peak performance**. The best description of being in the zone from an emotional place is calm concentration. If you can define it, you can go there. A calm, confident state of concentration is where you want to be.

Consider my approach to getting into the zone of peak performance. Any time you leave a place of calm concentration, you have left your ideal performance state. You want to learn to practice the art of creating and sustaining a state of calm concentration, no matter what you are doing. You could be cooking or cleaning. You could be exercising or studying. When you become aware that you're in a place of calm concentration, the mental-emotional state where flow happens, you can create a peak performance. Intentionally moving into the high-positive zone where your best performance happens begins with becoming aware of your emotions.

A million people were involved in a certain study. The researchers discovered that only thirty-nine percent of those million people could actually identify the emotion they were having when they were having it.

Consider the emotion of anger. Only thirty-nine percent of one million people, if they were experiencing anger, could actually identify their emotion as anger when it was happening. In some ways, that is alarming.

You must become aware of your emotions as you're experiencing them. Are you feeling depressed? Are you feeling excited? Are you feeling joyful? Are you feeling angry? Spend some time in a non-judgmental zone just to begin to get in touch with your emotion when you're experiencing it. You want to be able to identify your most empowering emotion. When you're doing your best, what emotion is connected to that? What is your most disempowering emotion?

Generally speaking, I've found that the most disempowering emotion for men is anger, while for females, it's inadequacy or fear—you don't believe you have what it takes to do it.

We want to get out of both of those emotions and move into a place of being confident, joyful, excited, and invigorated. The mark of a champion is someone who can turn a negative, disempowering emotion into a positive, empowering one at will.

If you're a competitive junior golfer, your physical and mental zone will most likely be more advanced than where you are emotionally. Being able to grab onto learning the emotional side of peak performance and generate the ability to intentionally move into a state of calm concentration as a teenager will set you far ahead of your peers. The competitive edge will be yours as you engage in your own personal formation in the emotional zone.

Perhaps you're someone who's farther along in your competitive journey, but your emotions have always been the one factor that's killed you in competition. If you will begin to study this grid and become self-aware, you will advance in your game. You'll begin to release and transform your negative emotions into positive emotions. You'll take a leap in your performance.

To echo the words of Tony Robbins about being a champion, "Your emotional state determines the quality of your life." Think about it. You could be on the backside of the desert, broke, and going nowhere, but if you're in love, guess what? Life is great.

On the other hand, you could have everything. You could be a millionaire. You could have achieved great things. Without joy in your life, though, life ain't so great.

If you can decide what your emotional state is going to be on the front end of your championship and walk in that, you are a champion. I believe that emotional mastery is critical, particularly in the culture we're living in. Everyone is whacked out with their emotions one way or another these days. You see it on the nightly news. Every day you can just decide, "I am going to be joyful." Joy is the highest emotion there is. For myself, I have made a decision. Regardless of what is going on in my life, I am going through it with joy.

Let me give you an example of how I do this. Sometimes the holidays can be a difficult time for me. I have a very small family, and I'm single. Sometimes during holidays I can start to slide into the low-negative emotional state and even depression.

A few years ago, I decided I was not going through Christmas and the holidays from a depressed state. I was going to make at least 100 families joyful. I ended up putting on a free webinar and shared how to make fresh connections with family. I reached 350 families with the webinar and witnessed a lot of transformation. This brought me great joy.

Somewhere along the way I got this really fun stuffed animal that I named Flame. When I put Flame in the passenger seat of my car, he looked like an actual live passenger. I can't tell you how many people stopped me at a red light, at the grocery store, and at the bank saying, "Who is that flamingo in your car?"

When I asked, "Do you want to meet Flame?" they said, "Sure." I produced all of this joy in people's lives just by taking Flame along with me on my holiday travels and spontaneously engaging them with my pink flamingo!

One day I was coming home from a get-together with family and friends, feeling a little down about something. When I stopped for gas, Flame was in the car. A man was standing against the wall at the convenience store. He took notice of Flame, saying, "Hey, I like your flamingo."

"Do you want to meet Flame?" I asked.

He said, "Sure." I took Flame out, and we sat there talking. We even made a Facebook post about it. The man looked over at me and exclaimed, "You made my day." We laughed hysterically over Flame as if he were real. Of course, sometimes I think he is.

It's a simple mental trigger for me to put Flame in my car during the holiday season or other special occasions. His presence is a reminder to remain in a state of joy.

Whatever performance you're going through, decide on the front-end how you're going to go through that performance. If you're a golfer, you'll decide ahead of time how you're going to play a hole and how you're going to swing the club. You have a crystal-clear swing-thought in mind. Now add the right mental-emotional state to your preparation. Determine how you are

89

going to "go through" your round, and then apply your ideal performance state to your game.

You can apply a positive emotional state to performances off the course, too. Many people today are going through a significant transition. Transition can be an extremely fearful place. I encourage you to go through it in peace and without fear. You may be a high school student searching out what college you will be attending. This could be a time of great anxiety and stress with your family. Don't go there. Be diligent and explore your possibilities in a state of excitement, not stress.

When you set up to compete in a tournament or championship, you must decide how to go through it. I encourage you to approach what's coming from a fearless place. Even when you take tests in school, how do you go in to take the test? Do you have an expectation of taking that test with fear? At a certain point, I said to myself, "I studied for my test in peace. I want to take that test in peace. Why should I change my emotional state if I have prepared for that test?"

Even though I was a top student, I was afraid to raise my hand in class. Finally I decided, "I am going to raise my hand in class. I am not going to be fearful, because I'm going through this in a high-positive state as a champion."

Again, it's important to be able to identify your most disempowering and empowering emotions. It is in that high-positive state that you're going to experience a peak performance. You want to guard that state.

I've often had to figure out how to turn that negative emotion into a positive one at will. After a tournament, I would be worn out. I had given my all—mentally, physically, and emotionally— to my performance. It could be very draining.

One of the greatest ways I learned to change my emotional state from that worn-out place was to jump in a swimming pool immediately after my round. By going into a place of play, it totally switched my energy and returned it to me. I found that I could empower myself just by deciding how I was going to use my recovery time.

I recall one situation where I was out playing in a competition all day. Afterward, I was feeling defeated and in a low-negative state. I walked into a

Whole Foods grocery store and was immediately struck with the refreshing environment. All around me were beautiful flowers, fruits, and vegetables. Classical music was playing in the background. I literally felt energy surging back inside me. I experienced a sudden shift from that grit-and-determined state—the hard-core athlete side of me— to the more feminine, the one that loved beauty. I morphed from a low-negative state back to a high-positive state. Making that U-turn has to do with choosing activities that bring fresh energy back to you.

You want to start becoming aware of what those positive and negative emotions are for you. In so doing, you can make choices for turning negative, disempowering emotions into positive, empowering emotions in your competitions. That's what true champions do.

In the next module, I will explain a process of debriefing after your competitions that can return you to that high-positive state.

I received a testimony from a competitive junior athlete who learned how to turn disempowering emotions into empowering emotions at will. She had done all of her declarations and had determined to put on her game face. From the start, she decided to play in her competition from a fearless, determined state of calm concentration.

Let me share with you her story of victory that came about once she'd become armed with the new knowledge she'd learned in *The Champion's Way*. It's a beautiful testimony of a young competitor who discovered her high-positive emotional state:

"I set out excited to see what the day would bring and how I would play. No matter what happened, I knew I would do my best to handle it in the best way possible and stay calm, cool, and collected. I did just that! I remained focused the whole time. With each stroke, I gained more and more confidence. Nothing could rattle me. My new dedication and approach led me to shoot the best round of my life. It was one of the best feelings in the world for me, and it was not all about the score. I felt the greatest sense of pride in knowing that I had used my new skills to believe in myself and stay positive throughout the whole round. It was like nothing I ever experienced before in a round of golf.

"I never got overly mad about a shot or extremely nervous just playing while completely focused on my target and my game. Nothing else mattered.

I had my game face on. This is something that Coach Veronica and I worked on, in putting my game face on when it came to play in a tournament. It was a look of determination, focus, and aggression. It meant I was ready to play and score. With this face on, I was confident and poised. It was a sign to me to stay positive and passionate. This, combined with my declarations, made me feel unstoppable."

Wow! You go girl! I found it interesting that her mental trigger was her game face. Fully applying her declarations and mental trigger, she out-did her best game.

Continuing, she said, "I had a feeling of self-power and a confidence I never felt before. It was a feeling of great elation to know that I could accomplish something I previously thought was out of my reach. Through this experience, I learned that I was capable of keeping a level head throughout my whole round. I saw that I was capable of shooting a low round. It was amazing to know I had done this, even more so because of the challenges I had faced on the way and how I dealt with them."

She went on to have an amazing high school season that far exceeded her expectations. Creating a result beyond your expectation in record time is completely possible for you, too, once you fully engage in *The Champion's Way* and unleash your empowering emotions!

MODULE 8 WORKSHEET

1. We all have empowering and _____ emotions.

2. Write down the emotions that fall under each category.

High Negative   High Positive

_____   _____
_____   _____
_____   _____
_____   _____
_____   _____

Low Negative   Low Positive

_____   _____
_____   _____
_____   _____
_____   _____
_____   _____

3. Peak performance takes place in which zone? _____

4. The best description emotionally of being in the zone is calm

_____

5. Any time you leave a state of CALM CONCENTRATION, you leave _____ performance.

93

6. When you leave CALM CONCENTRATION, the good news is, once you become aware of that, you can _____ to calm concentration.

7. What is your most empowering emotion?

8. What is your most disempowering emotion?

9. Champions can turn a disempowering emotion into an empowering emotion at _____.

10. Your emotional state determines the quality of your life. What is your predominant emotional state when you play golf (or other sport)?

11. You have the power to create your own emotional state and decide to play from that state FROM the start of your competition. Describe an upcoming challenge or competition that you are facing. Write out how you will go through that challenge staying in a high-positive state. Describe in detail what disempowering emotion you will guard against and the empowering emotions you will commit to creating from the start of your performance:

12. How do you "let go" of negative emotions?

13. What would it mean to you to play from a place of total emotional freedom?

THE CHAMPION'S WAY

MODULE 9

The Emotional Zone, Part II:
The Power of Debriefing

In this module we're going to explore how to achieve emotional mastery through the power of debriefing. I cannot emphasize enough the absolute importance of spending time to debrief a performance. Whether you're in a sport, in school, in the marketplace, or the arts—whatever your personal goal is, hear me on this. Emotions from a performance have to be completed. Otherwise, you'll take any negative emotions that you had from your performance into the next one because the energy of an emotion just doesn't disappear. It stays in you unless you deal with it.

You must debrief your competitions and performances so you can resolve any disempowering emotions and keep your ideal performance state free and clear. I call this process "bringing emotional completion" to your inner game. Then you can move on freely to your next performance.

How you leave something is how you enter the next thing. I know this. When I went home after losing the West Penn Amateur, my mom was on the bed crying. Instead of being able to deal with my state of mind, I ended up helping her with hers. No one was there to help me process the intensity of my own emotions.

A year went by. That experience had such a negative psychological effect on me that I actually forgot to turn in my application form for the next year's championship. I had completely blocked out the emotion of defeat, the negative impact from my failed competition. That was profound to me. A spirit of defeat not only affected me at the time. Quite frankly, it settled into me and stayed there for years because I did nothing to process it. I didn't even know I needed to address the emotional aftermath. I only discovered the necessity of processing emotions decades later.

If you are a coach, a parent, or a competitive athlete, you want to be sure that you go back and debrief the competition soon after it's done. That way, any negative emotional energy is completed and no longer stays inside you. If there's no way for it to escape, that thing will get inside your cells and become a part of who you are. You clearly don't want that to happen. If your experience was a positive one, it's still important to capture the feeling of success so that you can replicate it in a future competition. After I won my first senior championship a few years ago, I reflected on how much fun it was to win. Capturing the feeling of fun was an emotion I wanted to take into my future performances.

What does it mean to debrief a competition? It means you work through the competition and reflect on your performance in each of the zones. You want to do it in a place where you're calm, where you can think, and where you're looking back at it in hindsight. Don't do it too far out, though. You could let a day or two go by, but no more than that. Go back over it while the competition is still fresh in your experience. Ask yourself a series of questions.

I will include a debriefing sheet that you can use at the end of this chapter. Go through it. It's simply a series of questions to help you process your competition, to pull out the real learning point, and the real win from it. In terms of learning, there is always a real win in every competition, no matter what your score is. (Also see Appendix B for a debriefing worksheet.)

Here's the other reason why learning to debrief is such an important factor on your road to championship: you're going to fail a lot more than you will win. I want you to get the win of the process. In fact, you must get the inner win to score better in the next competition. I want you to get the win in the area of personal growth.

Here's the essence of the process: identify the inner win, whatever that learning point is, and then release the rest of it. All of it. It doesn't matter. All you need to take from your performance is what is going to serve you in the next performance. Let the rest go! Good or bad. Detach from it. Let it go!

Unless you debrief, you're not going to retain the knowledge of what you really learned. If you can get into a learning mode about your performances, you'll greatly decrease your sense of failure and defeat. You are giving meaning to the process of your performance, extracting from it the things you did do well and what you learned.

Helping a player to debrief is one of the greatest things a parent or a coach can do for him. Instead of criticizing, coach to debrief. Pull out that champion point, make it part of the next competition, and let everything else go.

Here are some of the questions in my basic debriefing sheet in this program:

What did I do really well today? I always ask my players first, "What are you really proud of?" You did some things really well. I am sure you did, even if it was that you showed up to play and you got in the game.

What one thing in each of the following categories can I work on to improve for the next match? You can go through the four champion zones: the physical, mental, emotional, and spiritual. Based on the process that you defined for yourself in each one, and the score you gave yourself when you began that process, how many notches did you go up or down?

Maybe you went from a three to a five. You can look at what you did and then set another goal— "I'm going to go from a five to a six." Ask yourself, "How am I going to do that?" "I'm going to work on this practice routine a little bit more," or "I'm going to do a little bit more of my core exercises." You are going back, tweaking and adjusting versus letting everything be a "win" or a "loss." Debriefing is very powerful. You will see the components of your performance in a way that you didn't see on the front end. You will gain a great deal of self-knowledge by working this process. You'll also gain a competitive advantage over others who are not growing in the area of self-awareness.

What was my best shot? What was my worst shot? You could also consider, "What were my mental errors?" Go back and examine that. Was it a matter of a skillset that you didn't have, a mindset, or what I call getting off your assets? Was it a matter of practice to really hone that skill? Discern the performance component that contributed to that outcome. Be specific. Get clarity. Clarity is power!

Here are other questions:

What did I learn about performance today?

What did I learn about myself today?

What did I learn about my sport today?

What did I learn from watching one of my playing partners?

How long did it take me to let go of a bad shot?

What was the real win that I'm taking away from this performance?

Once you debrief, then you will need to find a way to let everything else go.

It might be a simple reward system that affirms you. I love to give out little trophies. You can buy them at the dollar store. Get yourself a pack of them and give yourself a trophy for every process that you did well. Rewarding yourself with a trophy is a great way to affirm all the good things you accomplished.

I had a friend who rewarded himself after a successful study session. When he got through two hours of a productive study session, he would reward himself with half a Popsicle. Any small thing that's affirming will do the trick. You might want to go out to dinner with your family and friends. You may want to put your scores in an envelope or box to release them.

Whatever you do, you want to be sure that you debrief your competition. Be sure you process it and learn from it. When you make a practice of debriefing by asking yourself a series of questions, you'll be bringing your mind and emotions back to a place of peace. Remember again, emotions have to be completed after a competition.

Here's an example of the power of debriefing. I was coaching an Olympic hopeful one time. Because she had missed qualifying for the Olympics in track and field by less than half a second, she had missed the Olympics. Can you imagine training for years and then missing the Olympics by a fraction of a second?

It was three years after her qualifying heat that she came to me. I helped her go through *The Champion's Way* debriefing process. We went deep into her experience. Nobody had helped her process the whole thing to where she could find the real win and let it go.

When she processed and completed her defeat emotionally, she was able to get on with her life. Up until then, she had been stuck for three years because a spirit of defeat settled into her. It was not released because she didn't have anyone to help her process that competition. You really want to do that all along the way. You will grow by leaps and bounds as you do that.

I want to give you two more examples of debriefing a competition. The first has to do with academics. I had an eighth-grade student once who was struggling with ADD-ADHD. He had high-level, high-achieving parents. Each had a PhD. He was making D's and F's in school, but he really loved soccer. I was going through the emotional zone with him.

I drew a soccer field, and I put him in the middle of the field with a little stick figure. I asked him, "Where is your mom on this field? Is she on the field? Is she in the stands? He drew a little stick figure of his mom right on top of him.

He said, "My mom is on top of me emotionally! She even corrects my papers and rewrites them. It's killing me!"

I asked him, "Do you want me to go talk to your mom?"

"Yes," he said.

When I talked to his mom, she said, "Just shoot straight with me."

"You are killing your son. You're so concerned, you've slipped into being a helicopter parent. You are so on top of him that you're crushing his emotional space. He needs an emotionally-free space to be able to perform."

She broke down crying and confessed, "You're right. I have been so afraid that he's going to fail that I had to step in and perform for him."

She went to him and asked for his forgiveness. We mapped out a simple accountability system that freed him up to take ownership of his own emotional space. The system also made room for him to be accountable to his mom. We put a check list on the refrigerator. He filled it out when he completed his assignments. Immediately, he went from F's to B's after we created emotional space between him and his mom. We were able to debrief his assignments and make sure she kept that space clear by not encroaching upon it. Then he was able to excel academically.

The concept of honoring emotional space is so critically important, whether you are the person debriefing or you are trying to help coach someone. Often parents squelch a player's emotional space instead of protecting it. It's a critical component of one's ideal performance state.

Back when I was trying to qualify for the Women's U.S. Open, I was feeling like a failure from a previous failed performance. I went to my coach, who said, "Veronica, we are going to do this again, but we're going to pursue it in a different way. We are going to define this championship as fully engaging your heart in the process of preparing for a championship." I had to do my fitness goals. I had to work up to walking eight miles a day to be prepared for the qualifying round. I had to work on my swing. I did all my processes. In addition, I encouraged some friends to come along the ride to support me emotionally.

The day of the qualifier, I had a kidney stone attack. The temperature was a sweltering ninety-five degrees. I was so physically drained that I had to withdraw after the first eighteen holes. Here's the amazing thing: I had absolutely no negative emotions. There was no letdown, no defeat, not one disempowering emotion. Because of the way I defined success from the start, I eliminated the possibility of defeat. When I debriefed my competition, I saw that I was completely successful, because I fully engaged my heart in the process of preparing for a championship. The fact that I had to withdraw due to illness made no impact on me emotionally whatsoever. I was stunned to make this discovery.

What appeared to be failure was an absolute success. I was able to take the success of being "wholeheartedly faithful to my processes" into my next championships, to define them, and describe them in a way that would largely eliminate failure and defeat.

That is what *The Champion's Way* is all about. It's that holistic approach to peak performance where we are creating an atmosphere of growth. When there is a defeat or a failure, we can transform it into learning points that will help you to succeed.

I'm going to share one last example that I think is very powerful. In sports, when you don't have a coach, it's important to have peer mentors.

With peer mentors, you can talk about your competition together and debrief one another.

One day I was debriefing a competition with one of my students. When we were done focusing on her play, I asked her to reciprocate. "Hey, let's debrief my round with you today. Tell me what you thought." I invited her to coach me.

She was quick to observe. "Coach Veronica, you hit some really good shots. Every now and then, however, you hit a shot way out the wazoo. I have to wonder where it comes from." That remark convicted me to the point that I did not want to hit those shots anymore. I left that day thinking, "I'm going to fix my swing."

I thought about who could really help me fix my swing after being freshly motivated into action from my own student! I scheduled a lesson the next day after the debriefing. Within one hour, I understood how to fix the part of my swing that I had been working on for years. It was through the debriefing process with a peer mentor that gave me the impetus to say, "I am going to come up higher. I am going to get that thing fixed." It opened up a new possibility for me to move forward, and it all happened as a result of a debriefing session with my true champion student!

I think one of the greatest places of learning happens through debriefing, in learning to reflect on your performance. Instead of rejecting a less than acceptable performance, why not process it, get the real win from it, so you can accept it and move on? One of the best ways to debrief is to write a story about your competition. It's through writing that you process so much of your mental and emotional space. Writing helps you to integrate the parts of your experience into a coherent place in your brain. Integration brings wholeness. We want to create a really strong champion in you. To do that, you have to be a whole person.

Through writing about your performance, you will create a story. I often say, "Competitors have scores, but people have stories." You will have a story that you'll be able to take with you. It is amazing to me that here I am, decades after so much of my professional career is behind me, and what is it that am I sharing with you? My stories. You will always have the power of story to carry you along the road to championship.

In sum, learn to debrief. Go through *The Champion's Way* debriefing sheet and work on your emotional mastery. There IS a champion in you. You are working on achieving a peak performance. Debriefing is a vital tool that's going to empower you along your way. You just need to become clear on turning a disempowering emotion into an empowering emotion at will through the power of debriefing your competition, gaining the win, and letting the rest go!

I'm giving you an assignment. Select a recent competition to debrief. Take some time, at least thirty minutes, and give some focused thought on answering the debriefing questions. See what you uncover and learn about yourself!

To help you, here is an example of a debriefing from a Champion's Way junior golf student of mine:

1. What was the highlight of your competition?

   My highlight of my competition was how all my hard work paid off and I finished in the top three in the state!

2. What was the lowlight of your competition?

   The lowlight of my competition was that I was having difficulties dealing with the cold and all the wind, but I think I ended up adjusting to it pretty well.

3. What was your best shot?

   My best shot was on #10, which was one of the more stressful holes for me. I hit my 5 wood onto the green and ended up making the putt for birdie on day one.

4. What kind of shot did you most struggle with?

   I struggled with my approach shots the most, because I had a hard time keeping them straight.

   However, I learned to work with them.

5. What did you learn about yourself through this experience? About golf?

Through this experience I learned that I really do have what it takes to be a great player. I just need to focus on the right stuff and use the correct tools. Through this experience I learned that in golf, your attitude really does make a huge difference in how you compete and play. Having a good attitude can save many strokes. It allows you to recover from a not-so-good hole. It can make you feel better about yourself when you play.

6. What did you learn about being a champion through this experience?

Over the last few days, I learned that being a champion doesn't necessarily mean you have the best swing or you hit it the farthest, but having the right mindset can mean you are a champion. Walking and playing with confidence, having the ability to overcome troubles on the course, and overall being happy when you play, makes you a real champion.

7. What was your experience like playing in the last group on the second day? What did you like about it? To what extent did you feel comfortable in that place?

I really enjoyed playing in the last group on the second day. I felt a little nervous on the first tee, but I feel like I handled it pretty well. The girls I played with didn't really talk to me, so I just did my own thing, which was fine with me. I felt really comfortable throughout the round and hit some pretty good shots. On the last hole, on my approach, I felt pretty nervous. I looked up and saw all those people and I felt a little scared. I feel like I hit a pretty good greenside bunker shot. I was pleased with my bogey to shoot a 79.

8. What was your "greatest leap" in *The Champion's Way* process? Which zone did you feel you excelled the most in?

I feel like I excelled most in the mental zone. During my rounds I felt very relaxed, and I feel like I had relaxed concentration. I went from being worried and not focused to being confident, very relaxed and calm, and very focused on every part of my game.

9. What was the most valuable thing Coach Veronica said to you during your coaching time with her?

The most valuable thing Coach Veronica has said to me in my coaching time with her was that I really do have what it takes to be a great player. Also, if I'm in the right state of mind and if I just believe in myself, anything I set my mind to is possible.

10. How will you mentally prepare in the future for interruptions in your pacing?

In the future, I will mentally prepare for interruptions in my pacing by taking more time to get to my shot, reading my yardage book more, stretching in between shots to stay loose, and maybe thinking about other things than golf so I don't over-think the shot I'm about to hit.

11. What did you learn from your playing partners?

From playing with my partners, I learned that you should not get caught up in how they behave. If I'm playing with someone who gets very angry, it is in my best interest to stay away from her and think about myself. Someone's misfortune in how they play shouldn't cause me to play badly as well.

Now it's your turn!

MODULE 9 DEBRIEFING WORKSHEET

You can use the following debriefing template to process each of your performances. I recommend that you make a copy of this debriefing worksheet for each performance you have. Put them all in a notebook so you have a reference of your progress.

Name of Competition _____

Date _____ Score _____

1. What did you do really well today? What three to five things are you proud of?

2. What ONE thing in each of the following categories can you work on to improve for the next match? OR, What were your mental/emotional/physical/ spiritual errors?

   a. physical (technique, fitness, nutrition, energy)

   b. mental

   c. emotional

   d. spiritual

3. What was your best shot?

4. What was your worst shot?

5. What did you learn about performance today?

6. What did you learn about yourself today?

7. What did you learn about your sport today?

8. What did you learn from watching one of your playing partners?

9. What did you learn about loving yourself or others today?

10. How long did it take you to let go of a bad shot?

11. What is the one "win" (learning point) that you will take from your competition into your next competition? (This is your inner win.)

12. How did you demonstrate your higher purpose for playing/ mission today?

13. "I will embrace my inner win and release everything else and let it go by doing the following RELEASE IT ALL NOW ritual to complete my competition emotionally:

14. Competitors have scores. People have stories. An effective way to PROCESS a competition is to write a story about your competition. Describe your story and the real win you took from the experience:

THE CHAMPION'S WAY

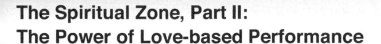

MODULE 10

The Spiritual Zone, Part II:
The Power of Love-based Performance

In a previous module, I defined the spiritual dynamics of performance as identity, higher purpose, and values. In this module, we are going to add the power of love as foundational to peak performance.

Consider this truth: anything spiritual is relational. *The Champion's Way* is a deeply relational approach to performance. It's critical that we learn to perform from a place of relationship. When you begin to perform outside of relationship—where all that becomes important is the goal—you begin to separate yourself from connection to your heart. Everything becomes focused on "that thing out there." The goal, not your personhood, begins to determine who you are.

You can get so wrapped up in the outcome that you actually separate yourself from yourself in the pursuit of your goal. You eventually get all wrapped up in performance-orientation. Performance-orientation is a deadly spiritual condition. It robs you of your truth worth. You lose who you are. Your worth becomes determined by how you perform. When you're so driven to achieve, you lose your sense of self in an obsession with the goal, creating a damaging crack in your foundation. Such was my downfall.

My father died when I was fifteen. I didn't really "know" him; that is, what made him tick. He was a hard worker but never spent any quality time with me. I cannot remember him saying, "I love you." I knew he did, but I never received any nurture from him or my mom. When he died, no one comforted me by saying they loved me, nor did I ever receive a hug from my mother. We never spoke about his death after the funeral. The day after he died, I had to go back to school. I just remember having to get 100 percent on my history exam. In the place where I needed nurture, I turned instead to achievement. Turning to achievement set off a whole lifetime of dysfunction. In order to have worth, I had to achieve something—and that something was never enough to fill the void of my self-worth.

The trap of performance-orientation is that it looks deceptively good on the outside. People were impressed with my graduating as the valedictorian of my high school. I was the first girl from my high school to get an athletic scholarship to college. Attending Duke University as a star student athlete was a highly impressive achievement. All those accomplishments made me shine. However, I was fractured on the inside. I was lost. I needed to know I was loved totally apart from my achievements. Nobody ever told me my worth had nothing to do with my accolades and scores.

I remember caddying for a little champion just seven years old in a world championship. He triple-bogeyed the first hole. He stood behind the hole and yelled out, "I hate myself. I hate myself. I hate myself." He defined his worth by his score. After the round, I spoke with his father with great concern about what I'd heard. Unfortunately, his father didn't get just how severe his son's performance-orientation was.

As a parent, a coach, or a player, what role does achievement play in the defining of self-worth? I often ask parents, "Are you raising a goal or a soul? Who is it that you're becoming? What is it that you're really creating on your road to championship? A whole person? A great competitor who is fractured as a person? How is your sport and your performance in it causing you to become a better person? Is your sport serving you, or are your serving the idol of sports?" The whole idea of mission is this: "I have a greater purpose, a greater end, and a greater vision than just the result." Again, you want to be sure that you are working on your values, because your values are what keep you grounded and centered.

The antidote to performance-orientation is love-based performance. In love-based performance, the person's value has nothing to do with his score. He is a valuable person just because he exists. When a player is loved, he is free to succeed and free to fail. Tiger Woods said, "I was never afraid to push my limits or to fail, because I always came home to love." There should be enough relational deposit, enough support from parents, family, friends, and coaches, that any defeat is swallowed up in acceptance. According to Kyle Rote, Jr., a great world-class athlete, "Sports is a wonderful tool but an awful god." We don't want the sport to own us; we want to own the sport. Love is the relational glue that keeps an athlete or a performer whole.

The following is a more specific comparison between a performance-based and a love-based approach to peak performance:

Doing vs. Being

Something that is performance-based is centered on the doing of something. It is based on results, productivity, goal-orientation, scores and achievement. In a love-based approach, your worth comes from the being side of life. You are a person apart from your performer self. In other words, your doing comes from your being. Your being does not come from your doing.

Being has to do with connection, being loved, a focus on yourself as a person. Performance is based on results, and being is based on process. The process is growth-oriented, not just an end point.

Productivity vs. Fruitfulness

Performance is based on productivity, and being is based on fruitfulness. Performance is based on a goal, and being is based on a soul—you are a person. Performance has scores, being has stories and growth.

Achievement vs. Authenticity

Achievement is based on accomplishing things—doing. Authenticity is based on personal-growth—becoming. This is being who you really are apart from performance. The athlete may be a son or daughter, maybe a husband or a wife. We want to learn how to achieve peak performance, but from a place of relationship, from a place of being an emotionally healthy, whole person. This is what *The Champion's Way* is all about.

To be sure that you're being nurtured in your process of reaching peak performance, you must love yourself and receive love from others. You must also extend love to those you are raising and coaching to be high performers. Love is the only fracture-free foundation there is to raising a high-performing, whole person.

One time I was trying to qualify for the U.S. Open. However, I did not want to go about it alone. I had an idea of creating a caddy club, a support and encouragement group that would help me along my way. I invited eighteen friends to come join me on my journey. They would offer their encouragement, good wishes, and prayers for me along my way. Every Sunday night I would send them an email, telling them of my victories and my needs.

I invited both men and women, young and old, golfers and non-golfers, to join my caddy club. It was so amazing. By the time the qualifier for the U.S. Open rolled around, I had eighty people in my club. I was inspiring them, and they were inspiring me. There were times I would take a dip and get discouraged. Somebody would shoot me an email and it would lift up my spirit, sharing the exact words I needed to hear.

You can do this, too. I call it "the great eight." I encourage you to start a caddy club. It isn't important what sport you're in or what your performance is; invite at least eight others to come join you on your road to championship. With Facebook, Instagram, and other social media platforms, it's so easy to invite others to take part in what you're doing.

People love to be inspired. I remember sitting in airplanes, explaining to total strangers, "I'm pursuing this goal, and I started a caddy club." They would immediately ask me, "Can I be part of your club?" I didn't even know them. But there was something about the energy and the pursuit of a goal that other people were inspired by. I wanted to go after my championship from a place of relationship, encouragement, and love. It was a beautiful exchange of my inspiring others and inviting others to inspire me. A caddy club is the perfect antidote to the loneliness of being in an individual sport like golf.

The sign of a truly healthy person is someone who has the ability to give love and receive love. Of course, you want to be able to perform and achieve a goal. But you also want to be able to give and receive love, to be healthy in your soul as you go about pursuing that goal.

One of the greatest examples of love-based performance I've ever experienced happened during a stay in private housing while I was playing in one of my tournaments. It was after a hard day of competition. It was blistering hot, and I hadn't played well. I felt defeated and totally depleted. It was that feeling of being worn out, of giving everything I had, and coming up short.

The folks I was staying with were wonderful and incredibly loving. The husband, Richard, was a gourmet cook, and his wife, Karen, was an affectionate and loving person. When I arrived back at their place, Karen swung the front door wide open. Surrounding me with the biggest bear hug ever, she remarked, "We love you, Veronica." I literally felt all defeat, all discouragement, and all my depletion completely wash out of me, instantly! Karen's loving energy filled my worn-out being with a fresh spark of life. I could feel her love invading every cell of my being. I will never forget that moment. She then handed me a glass of wine!

Richard had cooked a delicious meal. As we sat out on the back patio and talked, they continued to pour love into me. Their love and relational deposits dissolved the sting of defeat from the intensity of effort as I'd thrashed through my sport.

Perhaps you are not the player, but a parent or coach in a competition. Always remember to be intentional about loving in the midst of calling somebody up higher. My coaching always comes from a place of belief and faith in my student with whom I speak the truth in love. If I have to say something truthful to a student, it is always from a place of love, acceptance, and belief in the person. You want to be sure the player knows that they are affirmed and loved. Even in the midst of a performance, as in the example I just gave, a competitor needs a love shower as much as a physical shower to reach a peak performance.

This is a basic introduction to the concept of love-based performance. There are many more dynamics in the spiritual zone that I have not talked about when it comes to peak performance. There are deeper, more destructive spiritual dynamics, such as rejection, abandonment, self-hatred, and self-abuse that poison the soul of a competitor. Unfortunately, these dynamics are prevalent on the road to championship. Their destructive force is nullified when we form our self-worth apart from our performance. We want to be sure that our worth does not equal our score. In fact, we want to be sure our worth has nothing to do with our score. Drill this truth home in your heart: you are not your score!

I want you to be free from performance-orientation to be free to perform— to succeed, and to fail and rise again!

Sometimes stuff just happens in life. You could end up lying with your head on a pillow and find you can't move because of an injury or illness. Should that happen, where will you find your worth then? I want you to receive your identity and your worth from a love-based place and be able to freely give love to others as well. That is *The Champion's Way*.

My prayer for you is that you would know the love of God. You have worth simply because your Creator made you. You are priceless. No score or championship win or loss can give or take away the fact that you are a child of the Master of the Universe!

MODULE 10 WORKSHEET

1. Anything spiritual is _____. *The Champion's Way*
   is a deeply _____ approach to peak performance. We
   are to perform _____ a place of relationship. When we
   perform outside of relationship, we separate ourselves from

   _____ _____.

2. Performance-orientation is a dysfunctional state of equating your worth
   with your performance.

   YOU ARE NOT YOUR SCORE. Describe what performance-orientation
   means to you. How are you performance-oriented? How does it show up in
   your sport?

3. Your _____ has nothing to do with your score.

4. Do you struggle with separating your worth from your score? Describe it.

5. Are you becoming a goal or a _____?

6. How is your competition causing you to become a better person? How will you use your sport for a higher purpose?

7. What does it mean to be love-based in your performance?

8. Your defeats should be swallowed up in ＿＿＿＿＿＿＿＿＿＿.

9. We don't want the sport to own us. We want to ＿＿＿＿＿＿ the sport.

10. Where do you get your worth from?

11. Something that is performance-based is:

    a. ＿＿＿＿＿＿＿＿＿＿＿＿＿＿＿＿＿＿＿＿

    b. ＿＿＿＿＿＿＿＿＿＿＿＿＿＿＿＿＿＿＿＿

    c. ＿＿＿＿＿＿＿＿＿＿＿＿＿＿＿＿＿＿＿＿

    d. ＿＿＿＿＿＿＿＿＿＿＿＿＿＿＿＿＿＿＿＿

    e. ＿＿＿＿＿＿＿＿＿＿＿＿＿＿＿＿＿＿＿＿

12. Something that is love-based is:

    a. ＿＿＿＿＿＿＿＿＿＿＿＿＿＿＿＿＿＿＿＿

    b. ＿＿＿＿＿＿＿＿＿＿＿＿＿＿＿＿＿＿＿＿

    c. ＿＿＿＿＿＿＿＿＿＿＿＿＿＿＿＿＿＿＿＿

    d. ＿＿＿＿＿＿＿＿＿＿＿＿＿＿＿＿＿＿＿＿

    e. ＿＿＿＿＿＿＿＿＿＿＿＿＿＿＿＿＿＿＿＿

13. One of the greatest ways to nurture yourself as a competitor is to create a caddy club, a support system for you along the road to championship.

Name eight people who support you that you would like to invite into your championship:

1. _____

2. _____

3. _____

4. _____

5. _____

6. _____

7. _____

8. _____

14. How will you inspire them? I encourage competitors to send an email once a week, most likely on Sunday night, sharing your victories, struggles, schedule, needs, and stories. If you are faith-based, you can also ask for prayer. Invite your friends to send their encouragements.

15. If you're on a team, how will you love and nurture one another as you proceed down the road to championship? What does it mean to give yourself and others acceptance and encouragement? How good are you at doing this?

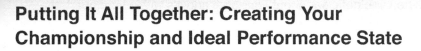

THE CHAMPION'S WAY

Putting It All Together: Creating Your Championship and Ideal Performance State

We have completed ten modules as it relates to *The Champion's Way*: Core Foundations for Achieving Peak Performance in Sports and Life. How do you put it all together?

Let me give you seven keys to peak performance. They are simple steps that encapsulate everything we've talked about. These steps give you a clear roadmap to putting all the ingredients together. Then we will create your own personal championship.

A holistic approach to peak performance requires that you have all seven keys in your strategy.

Key #1: A clear goal

The first key is that you must have a goal. Your goal might be to qualify for a particular competition, to reach a certain sales goal, to lose a certain amount of weight, to get a scholarship to college, to make the team, or to shoot a certain score. Regardless of what your goal is, you must have clarity about it. The goal is that target "out there," the thing that moves you forward. It's what presses you into a determined state to achieve it.

Many people don't have any goals. No matter where you are on your road to championship, pick a goal that inspires you and requires a full engagement for you to achieve it. I would encourage you to also approach your goal from a process-orientation. That way, it is something along a continuum. (Recall my desire to qualify for the Women's U.S. Open. That was my goal. My process-orientation toward reaching my goal was to "fully engage my heart in the process of preparing for a championship.")

Key #2: Commitment

Secondly, you have to commit to your goal. In other words, you must get the game on. You have to dive in, and you have got to be all in. You can't just say, "Well, that's a nice goal out there," and not go into sustained action to work toward achieving it. You have to be able to commit to it and become fully engaged. It has to be something that is true to you on the inside. What do you really want? When you get clear about your goal and it's within your heart, the commitment must match the desire.

Key #3: A coach

Thirdly, you're going to need a coach. A coach is somebody who helps you see things from a different perspective and who calls you up higher. She moves you along your way and helps clear away the obstacles. Your coach is someone more knowledgeable, skillful, and experienced than you. She is also someone who believes in you. Don't ever get a coach who offers only knowledge. You want a coach who offers you a real relationship, too. All great performers have coaches. Part of the key is finding a good coach. I wrote this book because I want to be one of your coaches. I believe in you. I also believe my journey, which has lasted over forty years, will help inform your path. I genuinely want to help you achieve peak performance and equip you on your journey. Even more, I want to empower you to become an even greater person.

Key #4: A system

Fourthly, you want to find an effective system, a way to go about what you are doing. If you're going on a trip, you need a way to get there. Nowadays, everyone uses GPS to map out their trips. As a technological system, it helps you get to your desired destination. The implementation of that system will help create the result you want.

The Champion's Way is an excellent system to use for obtaining peak performance. It's a framework of thought. It's more than a series of principles. It's a roadmap that, once you've learned it, can be applied to any area of your life. In fact, if you're a young person learning *The Champion's Way*, it will empower you to be set for life! I promise you!

Key #5: A deadline

You need a deadline. You also need a timeline. Deadlines are powerful. They pull you forward. They make you realize with certainty that you only have a certain amount of time to accomplish your process-oriented goals. Deadlines keep you in the game.

Personally, I always like to pick a championship every year so that I can work toward a peak performance. First, I pick the championship. Then I reverse-engineer it, breaking down my training into specific goals I want to achieve by specific timelines and deadlines. I always make sure I build in enough training time so I can achieve the necessary processes in order to be prepared in all the four champion zones to reach my goal.

Usually, I reserve several months for training. Once I determine my process-oriented goals and the timelines that go with them, I will go into superior focus mode. Often, it's not convenient, but it is imperative to chart your course with as much detail as possible. If you have a full-time job and a family, you have to make room for your championship. Championships are never convenient, but you can find the time for training if you're serious about your goal. If you're working full-time, perhaps you only have time for one championship a year. That's great, because the most personal growth you will ever experience as an adult is in the pursuit of a yearly championship where you set aside a few months to train and go for it.

In my championship training, the first month I always dedicate toward physical fitness, making sure I have the stamina, strength, and flexibility necessary for my goal. The second month I work on my swing mechanics. The third month I work on specific practice and playing goals. The fourth month I make sure I am in "full play" mode. Three weeks out, I stop all training on swing mechanics and work on being mentally and emotionally in my "calm concentration" mode, my ideal performance state. Because I also have job responsibilities, this is a championship plan that works well for me. I work the plan with a full commitment within the time frame I have. My coach, Jon, is a master at helping golfers determine what to be working on and when in the training process. He moves me along the road to championship!

If you're a young athlete, I encourage you to pick a championship that represents the highlight of your competitive season. For me, it was always a tournament in July when I would peak in my performance. Pick a big enough championship that inspires you to work toward it.

Think about how you can use smaller competitions as a strategy to leverage your performance improvement all the way up to your highlight competition. The reason why *The Champion's Way* is such a powerful system is because it is based on continual improvement. It's process-oriented, so you can take what you learned from each prior competition into the next competition with the aim of putting it all together in your highlight competition, whatever you've chosen it to be.

Remember, if you want to have a peak performance, you have to plan for a championship that is going to call you up into it. That's the beauty of a championship. It's something big enough that it calls all of you up into it.

We all have a championship. Maybe yours is athletic or academic. Perhaps it is to overcome an illness. Maybe it's a family or relational challenge. It could be a career change. The processes described here will equip you on your road to championship, regardless of what road you're traveling on. The steps involved will help you along your way.

Key #6: A caddy club support system

One of the most critical keys to peak performance is having adequate emotional support from others. Often, this is the most overlooked factor. Hear me on this: you need emotional support! You need people to come alongside you, who are there for you. You need a support system made up of people who are positive, who will help bring out the champion in you and provide that championship atmosphere for you.

Golf is my sphere, but it's just so darn independence-oriented. One of the things I'm trying to do in my sphere is create more community. People in community can come online or engage with you in person, sharing their thoughts and connecting together for mutual growth and enjoyment.

Golf is one of the greatest sports for comradery and friendship. I also think it should be a great sport for community, where people come together and collectively pursue champion development.

Make sure you develop your own caddy club support system when you design your championship. Regardless of the result, you will have impacted many lives! Write down who those people are. Send them an email and invite them to send you an email once a week. Give them your time frame so they'll know what's expected of them. If you have kids, invite them to encourage you!

Key #7: The reward

Finally, you need a reward. You need to say, "What will this do for me when I accomplish it?" For some, your best reward might just be the satisfaction of knowing you had significant development of your potential. You were able to do something you never thought you could do. For others, it could be a material reward or a relational reward. What is the payoff for all your hard work and effort?

Think about the reward you'd like to have. Feel it. What will make it worthwhile for you to pursue your championship, regardless of the outcome? Reasons are often related to reward, but not always. Choose a reward if you make the win. Or, choose a reward regardless of the outcome. For me, the reward is personal development and the chance to inspire others. It's the continual learning of peak performance. That's my "regardless reward." If I do win the championship, my reward is the feeling of accomplishment, of winning, and the fun feeling I get from it. I like collecting trophies, too!

Putting it all together

Now that you know the seven keys to a peak performance, you can go through them and create your own championship. It works for the pursuit of any kind of goal.

As you create your championship, take out the Champion Zone sheet. Flesh this out. You have four zones: the physical, mental, emotional, and spiritual. Put a name to your championship. What is it that you want to accomplish? What is your overarching goal? For example, maybe the overall goal would be to obtain a college scholarship.

Let us suppose you're a high school golfer and want to position yourself to get a scholarship and be a college player. That is a championship. It is personal growth-based. For this, maybe you could call your championship "College Player."

First, you would go into the physical zone and ask yourself, "Where am I now, and where do I need to be to put myself in a position to win a college scholarship?"

Perhaps your average score is 76 right now, but you know you need to average a 72. Average-wise, you're five strokes away from being eligible for consideration by the college you want. You must tell yourself, "What do I need to do different physically? Do I need to get help with my swing? Do I need to enter certain kinds of tournaments?"

Part of your "mechanics" may also involve the tactics of recruitment. You may need to ask, "Whom do I talk to with regard to being recruited?" There are mechanics to being considered for a college scholarship. You want to look at all of these things in the physical zone.

Next, in the mental zone, you might ask, "Do I have the work ethic that I need to put toward the effort for reducing my scores to get ready for a different kind of future? Am I an independent thinker? Can I function apart from my parents? Can I begin to call my own shots?" You want to think about what mindset development you need to do in order to accomplish your championship.

Let's go to the next zone. How do you need to grow emotionally? Do you need help with overcoming anger or strategies to prevent fighting against your parents? Do you need to develop confidence to contact an adult? Where do you need to be emotionally in this process?

Then spiritually, how do you see yourself? Do you see yourself as a college player? Can you see yourself winning tournaments or being a vital part of the team? How would a college player act, practice, study, and perform? Are you working on developing the identity and values of a college player now, while you're still in high school?

One of my true champion students was working on obtaining a college scholarship. When she got farther enough along in these processes, I said, "Now that you have your college scholarship, you want to play in such a way that when you get to college, you're not going to be hoping to play on a team, you're already going to be a strong college player. I want you to see yourself in that place now. Step into your college player identity now!"

Take your time to go through all your zones and create your processes for each one. They can be specific for now, or they can be a little broader.

You will notice on the zone sheet you have a scale of one to ten. Take a process. Let's just say for the physical zone, part of the mechanics is simply saying, "I have to identify five colleges that I would like to consider. I also need to find out what I need to do in order to be considered."

Then ask, "Where am I in terms of my courage to do that?" I might be at a 3. "What am I going to do this week to take my 3 to a 7? I'm going to research two colleges this week." Then you are moving up your "champ-o-meter" to accomplish your process. Be sure to identify a practice for each process so that practically speaking, you'll take action on executing your processes.

Follow this process for each one of your zones. You can continue to work on your zone sheet over a certain period of time. Go back and debrief. Go back and evaluate and update your zones on a weekly or a monthly basis.

Move yourself along as you create your championship. Then begin to execute it in all of the four zones. Whether it's an athletic, academic, or personal goal, you will then be working toward creating a peak performance. Be sure to have all seven keys in your plan as well. Anything less than all seven, and your peak performance will suffer. You need all seven!

Now you are fully engaged in *The Champion's Way*. It's a system that is personal growth-based, performance-based, and love-based. It will create the success you're looking for in a way that is ultimately beneficial to your well-being and to the integrity of who you are.

I began *The Champion's Way* with two pictures. The first one was about passion. It was there to open up your mind to new possibilities, to allow fresh passion and motivation to come forth from you. Then there was the picture that represented focus, the ability to take dead aim on a target. I spoke about creating processes and practices where passion and focus worked

concurrently, resulting in a leap in your performance.

You now know how to take your leap! The path—the way—has been laid out for you.

You can now pursue your goals and achieve the breakthrough wisdom that you need to realize the champion you were created to be. If I can be of further help to you, please reach out to me. Your champion development is the true prize of my life.

In the last module, I am going to share a couple stories that will profoundly inspire you along *The Champion's Way*.

MODULE 11 WORKSHEET

1. List the seven keys to a peak performance:

   a. _____

   b. _____

   c. _____

   d. _____

   e. _____

   f. _____

   g. _____

2. What key are you missing?

3. What key(s) are you strong in?

4. What is the championship that is in your heart? Write it down here:

5. What is your strategy or plan to put yourself into the energy of your championship now? Who is your coach? What is your system? What processes do you have to engage in to be ready for your championship? What is your timeline? Who will be your emotional support system? What is your reward?

    Flesh it out here:

6. Take out your Champion Zone sheet and fill out each zone with a process-oriented goal. Give yourself a score, which is largely subjective on a scale of 1 to 10, as to where you are right now. Determine a timeline where you will come back and measure your score. Perhaps it's over a week or two. Determine the practice behind each process to move you forward. Write it in each zone. Label your championship at the top of the page.

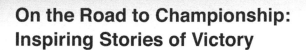

THE CHAMPION'S WAY

MODULE 12

On the Road to Championship: Inspiring Stories of Victory

Competitors have scores. People have stories. Long after you shoot a score, you'll have a story. It's the power of story you'll take with you on the road to championship that will convey your true greatness and inspire others.

Always make sure you build on your inner wins, regardless of your scores and results. Then you will be a true champion. Being a true champion has nothing to do with how many trophies you achieve. It's about forming and expressing the true champion within—who you are, including your character, your thinking at the highest level, and how you live your life with an excellent spirit.

Throughout your journey, be bold to share your story. Regardless of what stage you're at in your journey, there's always someone behind you who needs your inspiration. Give it to them. Inspire them while you are aspiring. Then you'll always have meaning to your efforts and passion. I want to dedicate this final module to inspiring the champion within you.

The following are two stories from my life. They come from my sport of golf and from my desire to live a champion's life. I believe being a champion in sport and life is about overcoming obstacles and setbacks. It is also about helping others to overcome their challenges as well. Both stories testify to the power of a championship. Normally, we consider a championship to be an athletic pursuit. In this program, we're also talking about how *The Champion's Way* can be used to empower your life.

You may be taking this training on the beginning trajectory of your life journey as a competitor, an athlete, an achiever. There comes a time, however, when you're going to face winds of adversity. The concept of a championship, of pursuing a vision "way out there" that's bigger than yourself, is a powerful way to move your life forward. When you're experiencing a setback, a championship can be the way to make an amazing comeback.

I have encountered many people whose championship is all about overcoming an illness. I know that was the case for me when I was about thirty years old. I had played the golf tour and then quit for five years. Deep inside, I still wanted to play. However, I wanted to find a way to play out of the freedom of who I was. I didn't want my sport to hold me hostage anymore. I wanted to be master over my sport. Since I didn't know how to do that, I quit for many years.

During that time, I went to graduate school and earned two master's degrees. I also prayed about my golf for those five years, wondering why I would be given a talent and have it taken away? I wanted to understand my inner struggle and be freed from it to enjoy golf as a game.

After graduate school, I decided to go back and pursue professional golf again. Things began to fall in place. I secured a sponsor and was soon back on the golf tour. However, I didn't have a lot of wisdom regarding energy management. I was so excited to be back playing again that instead of playing two or three tournaments and taking a break, I played in ten. Finally, at one tournament, I ended up crashing my immune system. I also found out later that many of the girls were affected by water poisoning at a tournament, which also affected me.

While on the second hole of a tournament in Manhattan, Kansas, I almost collapsed on the course. When I looked down, I saw two balls instead of one. Knowing something was very wrong, I withdrew from the tournament. Five doctors later, they diagnosed me with what is now known as chronic fatigue syndrome. I ended up in Tulsa, Oklahoma, staying with some folks that I didn't know, for a period of six months.

That was not my only setback. Tragically, my beloved golf instructor was killed in a plane crash. I landed in a town where I didn't know a soul, but where I had to recover. Everything in my life just came crashing down. I was bedridden for the most part of nearly three months.

Around Christmas time, I received an article about me from my hometown newspaper in Virginia. The story was full of negatives. I remember saying to myself as I was reading it, "This is not how I want my story to end. I do not believe I have come all this way for my golf journey to culminate in a negative story."

Being a person of faith, I decided to pray and activate my faith. As I prayed, I heard a small voice inside say, "Go for it." I thought, "Go for it? Go for what? I'm lying in bed. Everything has crashed. Go for what?" The only thing that came to mind was the U.S. Open in the upcoming year. It was the only tournament I could go for without actually playing on the golf tour.

I decided to pursue the U.S. Open championship by faith and to fully engage in it. First, however, I had to start walking. I thought, "Okay, the first thing I have to do is find a hill and climb it." That is pretty hard in Tulsa, because Tulsa is flat. Even so, I managed to find a small hill and climb it. Doing so required all the strength I had within me.

The next day I took another step. The following day, I took another step. Within a few months, I was jogging. All I could do was play a couple of rounds of golf a week. That's all the strength I had.

That spring I found a teacher who helped me with my swing. He gave me confidence, and I grew in the belief of my method. My faith grew, too. I still had no money and was not able to work. I also didn't have much motivation. All I kept hearing was this little voice that kept saying, "Go for it. Just do it." I listened to that voice. I stepped out on that voice. I focused on it and put trust in it. I was about the business of generating a new story for myself.

It was time for the practice round of the U.S. Open Qualifier held at Las Colinas in Dallas. While hitting balls on the driving range the day before the tournament, I stood next to a guy who was hitting balls, too. He was yelling at himself, "Oh, you jerk!" Then he hit some more balls and continued, "You are really terrible. What are you doing out here?" He kept expressing all this horrible self-talk. Then he turned around to me and remarked, "You look like you have it all together."

"Friend," I remarked, "You have no idea where I have been."

I ended up playing nine holes with him. As it happened, I was able to help him and coach him about his own life and attitude. At the end of those nine holes, I discovered my higher purpose for playing: to inspire other people, just as I helped this man with his life. It set me free to fail the next day because I had found a larger meaning for what I was doing.

For the second nine, I played with some lady professionals who would be in the tournament the next day. Somehow, I started playing worse than usual. Back in my hotel room that night, I went back to prayer. The question I wrestled with was, "Why did I play more poorly with those girls than with that guy?"

The answer came as quickly as I asked it. "You were playing out of a spirit of fear and intimidation."

I immediately invoked the power of declaration. I got so mad! I stomped around my hotel room shouting, "I don't care if I shoot a hundred tomorrow, I will not play out of a spirit of intimidation. That is not who I am. If I shoot a hundred tomorrow, it will be with gusto!"

I loudly declared to my atmosphere that I was going to play as a champion. I was going to play from victory regardless of my score. In the middle of my spiritual rampage, an extraordinary peace came over me. I just knew I was going to qualify for the U.S. Open the next day. I would not know how to describe it to you other than that. I just had a complete inner sense of knowing it was going to happen, so I went to bed and slept soundly.

The next day I went to tee off. My caddy's grandmother had died, so I didn't even have a caddy. I was able to get a guy from the caddy shack to help me. I hit my first shot "boom," right down the fairway. The second went "boom," right on the green. I made an easy par.

On the second hole, the same thing happened. By the third hole I am saying to myself, "Something is going on here!" My second shot hit a big mound. It should have turned right into the water. Instead, it turned left and landed right on the green about ten feet from the pin. By the fifth hole, I could hardly contain myself. I kept hitting all these great shots.

My caddy kept saying, "Come on, Veronica. This is a birdie hole." I would think four and he would think three. His encouragement and ability to know my game and the golf course were tremendous assets. By the end of that day, I had five birdies, shot 71, and won the Women's U.S. Open Qualifier. I was off to my first U.S. Open! There is no doubt in my mind that I received some major divine help that made it possible for me to do the impossible. From the sick bed to the U.S. Open in six months' time was an amazing comeback.

I had an incredible experience at the U.S. Open. While there, I also had the privilege of honoring my mother and the memory of my father during a speaking engagement. I didn't make the cut, but I was set free to play the game—the game that had held me in such a negative way. And now I was free to pursue golf as a game and to use my sport in any way I wanted to. It no longer defined me. I defined it. I was free to teach golf, free to use the game as a metaphor for life lessons. I was free to play, free not to play. It was such a beautiful and powerful story. It was a story of the power of a championship and of the power of faith. I accomplished something more by listening to the Voice that was speaking to the champion in me than in anything I could have done in my own effort. I made my comeback and have had the privilege of inspiring thousands with my story.

Let me encourage you. If your championship is one of overcoming an illness or overcoming a setback, don't let your history remain your story. The power of a championship is that it moves you into your future. You start pressing forward. You start thinking about using generative language, which means, "I will. This is where I am going to go. I am going to create." The opportunity to be fully engaged is what brings the energy back to you.

So many people who struggle with an illness allow their illness to define them, instead of their defining their illness and envisioning an outcome beyond the challenge. If you grasp what I am saying, you actually start living from the future back to the present versus the past to the present. All champions who have a championship envision themselves already there and start moving toward their envisioned future. I discovered this powerful dynamic in the pursuit of my championship. I did something that I considered to be absolutely impossible. Just six months prior, I could hardly lift my head off a pillow, yet there I was at the U.S. Open!

I encourage you: choose a championship. Do not be afraid to activate your faith in the process. You will discover you can do far more than you envisioned what's possible. That is *The Champion's Way.*

My U.S. Open story was one of learning how to speak to my inner champion. *The Champion's Way* is also about speaking to the champions in others. One of the most powerful truths I have learned about *The Champion's Way* is that true champions use their spirit, their story, and their platform to inspire other champions. I have one more story to share with you from my road to championship. To me, this is one of the most remarkable stories of my life about inspiring another champion. That person happened to be my mother.

My mother always thought the game of golf was stupid. She grew up in the Depression era and had to quit school in the fifth grade to earn a living. Anything that had to do with play was meaningless to her. Oddly enough, my mother turned out to be an amazing athlete that no one had ever discovered, including herself. All her life, she saw herself only as a scrubwoman and a housecleaner.

My mother didn't believe she was doing a good job unless she was sweating profusely after three hours of cleaning. I would always wonder, "What is it inside of her that drives her that way?" I began to see that my mother actually saw cleaning the house as an Olympic sport. She went after it with all of her tenacity and passionate effort.

At age eighty-five, my mother had a terminal heart condition. She was given just six months to live. I decided at that time to set aside my career and my own desires and dreams to reach my mother's heart before she passed away. Although we were in each other's lives my whole life, we were emotionally estranged. We had never really connected heart-to-heart.

I was getting a life coach certification at the time, and I really wanted to reach her. I bought her a dog and a cat. I took her around to old folks' homes, but everybody was too old for Mildred's taste. Finally, one day out of exasperation, I said, "Mom, that's it. I've had it. We are going to the golf course! Get your tennis shoes on. We are headed to the driving range."

To my surprise, she agreed to come. I handed my mom an eight iron. She took the club and began to waggle it. I said, "Mom, where did you get that waggle? I don't waggle the club."

"Oh, that's how pros do it!" she said.

"Mom! You're watching too much Tiger Woods!" I replied, chuckling.

After she waggled the club again, Mom took a big backswing and swung down on the ball with impressive force. She sent the ball sailing almost 100 yards on her first try! "Mom!" I exclaimed with shock, "I thought I got it from Dad." Forty years later, our eyes were both wide open with a new sense of wonder as we were in a moment of shocking discovery! Mom was a natural athlete!

I put another ball down. Mom took another signature waggle, followed by a big turn. Whack! The ball went flying 100 yards again. By this time my mother looked at me with fresh fire in her eyes. Here was a woman who had wanted to die. All her siblings had passed. She didn't think she had a reason to live. All of a sudden, her inner athlete—her inner champion—was activated. She looked at me and demanded, "Put another ball down!" That started my mother's golf career at age eighty-five.

It was amazing! Her very first round of golf was at Pine Needles. I'll never forget Mom strutting up to the first tee. It was the exact same tee from which all the Women's U.S. Open players had fired off their first shots earlier that year. My mother pranced up there with her little blue golf hat on and proceeded to waggle her rustic Patty Berg 3 wood. She took a big backswing and popped that 3 wood 150 yards down the center of the fairway!

I said, "Mom, what a great shot!"

"I know!" she retorted.

"Mom, hop in the cart. I will take you to your ball."

"I am not hopping in any cart. I am walking to my ball!" she exclaimed.

A little down the fairway, she took her 3 wood and proceeded to totally whiff it. At that point, she looked at me and said defiantly, "I am giving up this game. I should be better than this by now! I have practiced for a whole six months."

I replied, "Mom, it takes a little longer than six months to learn golf!"

It was so beautiful to see my mother swinging the club. We developed a perfect friendship on the golf course. The very sport that had kept us apart before this time now gave us an amazing connection and comradery. It also sparked in her a desire to live. The most amazing thing is, together we turned that six-month death sentence into seven fruitful years of friendship and memory-making.

At eighty-eight, and with my help, she started a housecleaning business and had her first paid modeling shoot. At eighty-nine, she started public speaking. At ninety, I told her it was time for her first golf tournament. I organized her first Grandma Open and brought together the generations. At ninety-one, my mother died my best friend. It was glorious. I have this picture of her at ninety years old, of Mom in all of her glory. I was able to see the champion in my her come forth. The woman who was dying was literally blossoming at the same time.

One time she told me that her stepfather made her give up playing basketball in the fifth grade because it scuffed up her one pair of shoes. I decided to remedy that. I went out and bought her a pair of bright pink Nike tennis shoes. I put them on her feet and said, "I'm going to help you run all the way to your finish line." That was my commitment to my mother. I spoke to the champion within her and committed to bringing her forth. And I did. To this day, I have more joy in sharing my mother's story than in winning all my trophies throughout my lifetime.

Let Mom's story be an inspiration to you, whether you're a young person at the beginning of your athletic career or you're at the end of your competitive journey. There is always more for you. You have many gifts and talents yet to be explored. You have to have faith all the way to the finish line. You cannot quit.

My mother blossomed at the end of her life because I spoke to the champion in her. The legacy she left me was the knowledge of who she really was: a great athlete, a communicator, a tenacious fighter, and a best friend I never had growing up. We went about the business of creating life. In doing so, we extended her life longer than anyone thought was possible.

If you're a senior citizen and there is still a spark inside you, I want to encourage you to step out and explore it. Gather your family and friends around you and invite them in. Ask for their help and involvement. The greatest gift you can leave your family is the knowledge of who you really are.

Your family deserves to see your champion self. The memories you will leave them of seeing your inner champion unleashed will keep their cup full for the rest of their lives! That's what my time with Mom did for me.

Not only did I inspire the champion in my mother, my mother inspired the champion in me. She inspired me to keep playing the game. I discovered the joy of playing it from a place of camaraderie and friendship. I realized in middle age that I could decide what golf was going to mean to me. I could pick a championship on a yearly basis and pursue it. It no longer had the same definition as when I was a young person growing up. I could turn it into an adventure with my own self-exploration and self-growth.

Something beautiful unfolded when I embarked on my championship journey with my mother. I was inspired by the champion I unlocked in her. Though she never won an athletic trophy, she was cut out of the same cloth as the great LPGA teacher and co-founder, Peggy Kirk Bell. Mrs. Bell did so much for the game of golf. She was a great champion in the LPGA and a great champion of life. My mother actually inspired Peggy Kirk Bell in her story to have faith all the way to the finish line.

Whether you end up being a well-known champion or whether you're a champion in life, *The Champion's Way* is a path for you to cultivate your best self. Whether you're fifteen years old on the start of your journey or eighty-five years old like my mom was, we can all speak to the champion in each other.

We can all come up higher.

The beauty of golf is that there is no generation gap in the game. Young and old can play the same game on the same course together. It will enrich your life tremendously if you make friends of all ages along your road to championship. Both young and old, we have gifts of friendship, wisdom, and joy to offer one another.

Always remember to "inspire while you aspire" along the road to championship by sharing your stories with others. By following *The Champion's Way*, we can enjoy the fullness of the game and the fullness of life together. That's the true victory of *The Champion's Way*.

MODULE 12 WORKSHEET

1. What "spoke to you" in the sharing of my U.S. Open comeback story or the story about my mom?

2. What does it mean to you to have "faith until the finish line"? What is your finish line?

3. What is your life championship—the one that is outside of your sport?

4. What is the new story you want to create for yourself?

5. All champions envision themselves already winning the championship—
   and working backwards to realize it. What is your championship? What
   will you do by faith?

6. Champions speak to the champions in _____.
   Do you have an inspirational story you would like to share to empower
   others? Write it down here. If you decide to send it into me, I will share it
   with others to inspire them. (Your sending it in is giving me permission to
   publish it.)

   You can send it to: veronica@truechampioncoaching.com.

Appendix A

The Champion Zones - Defining Your Process-oriented Goals

Physical — swing mechanics/fitness/nutrition/energy management

1   2   3   4   5   6   7   8   9   10

Mental — focus/concentration/champion mindsets

1   2   3   4   5   6   7   8   9   10

Emotional — empowering vs. disempowering emotions

1   2   3   4   5   6   7   8   9   10

Spiritual — identity/ values/higher purpose

1   2   3   4   5   6   7   8   9   10

My champion challenge/championship is:

_____

_____

Veronica Karaman
TRUE CHAMPION
COACHING

Karaman © 2012

Appendix B

The Champion's Way Debrief

Competition _____

Date _____

1. What did I do really well today? What 3 to 5 things am I really proud of?

2. What ONE thing in each of the following categories can I work on to improve for the next match? OR What were your mental/emotional/ physical/spiritual errors? Go over one by one in detail.

    a. physical _____

    b. mental _____

    c. emotional _____

    d. spiritual _____

3. What was my best shot?

4. What was my worst shot?

5. What did I learn about performance today?

6. What did I learn about myself today?

7. What did I learn about my sport today?

8. What did I learn from watching one of my playing partners?

9. What did I learn about loving myself or others today?

10. How long did it take me to let go of a bad shot?

11. What is the one "win" (learning point) that I will take from this competition into my next competition?

12. How did I demonstrate my higher purpose for playing/ mission today?

13. I hold onto my "inner win" and release everything else and let it go by doing the following "RELEASE IT ALL NOW ritual to complete my competition emotionally:

Recommended Resources

The Champion's Way 12 Module Video Series by Veronica Karaman, jointhechampionsway.com

My Shot of Joy: A Miraculous Journey of Redeeming a Lost Mother-Daughter Relationship by Veronica Karaman

How Champions Think in Sports and Life by Dr. Bob Rotella

The Champion's Mind: How Great Athletes Think, Train, and Thrive by Jim Afremow, PhD

Finding Your Zone: Ten Core Lessons for Achieving Peak Performance in Sports and Life by Michael Lardon, M.D.

The Champion's Way by Steve Victorson, EdD and Robert L. Yehling

Mind Gym: An Athlete's Guide to Inner Excellence by Gary Mack with David Casstevens

Mastering Golf's Mental Game by Dr. Michael T. Lardon

The Power of Full Engagement: Managing Energy, Not Time is the Key to High Performance and Personal Renewal by Jim Loehr and Tony Schwartz

The Only Way to Win: How Building Character Drives Higher Achievement and Greater Fulfillment in Business and Life by Jim Loehr

The New Toughness Training for Sports by James E. Loehr, EdD

Heart of a Champion: True Stories of Character and Faith from Today's Most Inspiring Athletes by Steve Riach

Be a Player: A Breakthrough Approach to Playing Better on the Course by Pia Nilsson and Lynn Marriott

How Successful People Think by John C. Maxwell

About the Author

Veronica Karaman is a champion mindset coach and thought leader who has dedicated her life to helping others achieve their maximum potential in athletics, academics, and personal development from a place of wholeness.

Professional golfer, author, and speaker, she is the founder of True Champion Coaching, a peak performance practice where she offers both secular and faith-based trainings. Veronica is the author of six books, including the inspirational story, *My Shot of Joy: A Miraculous Story of Redeeming a Lost Mother-Daughter Relationship.*

A graduate of Duke University and Regent University as a Beasley Scholar, Veronica holds two master's degrees and is the recipient of numerous accolades and awards.

She still loves to compete as a senior golfer and is proud of winning the 2017 Tennessee Senior Women's Open by 13 shots!

For further information about *The Champion's Way* and Veronica's coaching, please visit: Jointhechampionsway.com (a Facebook platform) for *The Champion's Way* online video series.

For group or personal performance coaching with Veronica or to book Veronica for speaking engagements, please contact: **veronica@truechampioncoaching.com.**

To engage on social media:

www.Facebook.com/VeronicaKaramanCoaching

Instagram.com/veronicakaraman

Blog: veronicakaraman.com

(All links are current at the time of publishing.)

Acknowledgments

I am grateful to my father, who introduced me to golf, the game I love for life. Thanks, Daddy. To my mom, who brought me back to the game at age forty when I ended my touring years. You taught me the joy of playing the game not to compete, but to connect heart-to-heart. I will never forget laughing down the fairway with you. To Jon Corliss, my lifelong colleague and performance coach. You always motivate me to enter one more championship.

I am grateful to Dr. James Loehr, whose performance wisdom on stress-recovery cycles helped me heal from seventeen years of chronic fatigue. Your teachings on the power of full engagement echo throughout this book. Thank you for the profound impact you have made on my life.

To Dr. Joseph Umidi, thank you for your transformational coaching. The training I received through Life-forming Leadership changed my life forever and helped shape the relational-based approach to performance found in these words. You taught me that we are whole only when we can both achieve and relate. Acquiring the tools for listening and asking powerful questions are what help me unlock potential in others in an accelerated and powerful way.

To my Caddy Club, my personal support group who have encouraged, inspired, and prayed for me throughout all my championships. You're the best!

To all the students and their families whom I've had the privilege to coach in *The Champion's Way*. Thank you for your trust, your stories, and your pursuit of excellence.

To my graphic designer, Patrick Wright. You always capture the essence of my words in the perfect image. To my editor, Suzanne Rhodes, thank you for your thoroughness and heart for my writings.

Most of all, I have quit too many times to not acknowledge the one person who believed in me when I didn't believe in myself.

From the start, you were there when I didn't have a father. You guided me to Duke University when I didn't even know what Duke was. You led me to every sponsor and teacher I ever had. You walked down the fairway with me, taught me how to fight, how to win, and how to face the dark side of the game. You placed your hand in mine and held it until I found the light of victory.

You taught me how to recognize my critical and judgmental voice—and then slay it. You taught me how to cultivate my coaching voice and never stop forging through to my champion voice. You instilled in me a relentless pursuit of unlocking potential in myself and others.

You taught me to love my sport, to love myself, to love others, and to love you in the game.

Every time I needed to lay it down, you let me. Then you took me by the hand and whispered time and time again, "Let's tee it up again. You're not through. I have more to show you."

It's been a long walk down the fairways with you. In this moment, all the treasures of knowledge and wisdom over a lifetime have come together to become broken bread and poured out wine for others. I've come to realize there is one more voice in peak performance. It's beyond the champion voice. It's the championing voice—the one that advocates for others. It's the one that sends out a clarion call, "This is the way, walk in it!" Thank you, my Lord Jesus Christ, for the call to mentor others in *The Champion's Way*.

Thank you for the high calling to each of us to be true champions:

"Do you not know that in a race all the runners run, but only one gets the prize? Run in such a way as to get the prize" (I Cor. 9:24).

Made in the USA
Middletown, DE
25 January 2023

21936148R00093